The Anglican Covenant

The Anglican Covenant

Unity and Diversity in the Anglican Communion

Edited by

Mark D. Chapman

mowbray

Published by Mowbray
A Continuum Imprint

The Tower Building   80 Maiden Lane, Suite 704
11 York Road   New York
London SE1 7NX   NY 10038

www.continuumbooks.com

First published 2008

British Library Cataloguing-in-Publication Data
A catalogue record for this book is available from the British Library

Typeset by the author
Printed and bound in Great Britain by MPG Books Ltd, Bodmin, Cornwall

ISBN 10: 0–567-03253–1 (paperback)
ISBN 13: 978–0-567–03253-9 (paperback)

Contents

Foreword

This collection addresses the proposed Anglican Covenant
from a variety of perspectives. It aims to survey recent
development in the Anglican Communion in the context of
history, theology, and biblical interpretation. Although most of
the chapters emerged from a conference organized under the
auspices of Affirming Catholicism at St Matthew's Church,
Westminster on 20 January 2007, the contributors represent
different Anglican viewpoints, both ecclesiological and
cultural. The Conference was designed to encourage people to
come together in a spirit of open dialogue. I am most grateful
for the honesty and humility displayed by all the participants
and contributors, and for their willingness to listen to one
another. Five of the chapters published here (chapters 1, 2, 3, 4
and 6) began as papers presented to the Conference. The
others offer understandings of covenants and their implications
from theologians outside the Anglican Communion (chapters
7 and 8), from a leading British Old Testament scholar
(chapter 9), and from a prominent church historian (chapter 5).
I hope that the book will offer insights and resources to assist
the Anglican Communion in its task of finding a way out of its
current difficulties.

Thanks are due to Thomas Kraft of Continuum for
supporting the project from the outset, and to the Revd
Richard Jenkins and Lisa Martell, Director and Administrator
of Affirming Catholicism for planning the Conference.

Mark D. Chapman
The Feast of Alban the Martyr, June 2007.

Notes on Contributors

Victor Atta-Baffoe studied at the Episcopal Divinity School in Cambridge, Massachusetts, and took his STM at Yale Divinity School in New Haven, Connecticut. He completed doctoral studies at King's College, London. He is currently Dean of St Nicholas Seminary, Cape Coast, Ghana, where he teaches Doctrine and Liturgy. He is a member of the Inter-Anglican Doctrine and Theological Commission and is also Chairperson of The African Network of Institutions of Theological Education Preparing Anglicans for Ministry (ANITEPAM). Victor also serves as a member of the Anglican Covenant Design Group.

John Barton is Oriel & Laing Professor of the Interpretation of Holy Scripture in the University of Oxford and a Fellow of Oriel College. He is the author of a number of books on the Bible, including *People of the Book? The Authority of the Bible in Christianity* and *What is the Bible?*, as well as co-editor of the *Oxford Bible Commentary*. His latest book is *The Nature of Biblical Criticism* (2007). He is a priest in the Church of England and assists in the parish of Abingdon. He is also a member of WATCH, and was a member of the General Synod from 2000 to 2005.

Mark Chapman is vice-principal of Ripon College Cuddesdon, Oxford, and a member of the Faculty of Theology at Oxford University. He is a Church of England priest and serves as honorary assistant curate at All Saints' Church, Cuddesdon. He has published widely in the fields of church history and many other aspects of theology. His most recent books are *Blair's Britain: A Christian Critique* (2005), *Anglicanism: A Very*

Short Introduction (2006) and *Bishops, Saints and Politics* (T & T Clark, 2007). Mark is publications officer for *Affirming Catholicism* and co-editor of the *Journal for the History of Modern Theology*.

Gregory Cameron is Deputy Secretary General of the Anglican Communion, where he has responsibility for the international ecumenical relations and dialogues of the Communion, and for the process arising out of the Windsor Report 2004. He is Secretary to the Covenant Design Group, which has been charged by the Instruments of Communion with developing the draft text of the Anglican Covenant. He is a student and teacher of Canon Law, and was awarded an honorary Doctorate of Divinity by the Episcopal Divinity School in Cambridge, Massachusetts in 2007, for his ministry of reconciliation in the Communion.

R. William Franklin is Academic Fellow and Associate Priest of the Anglican Centre in Rome and Associate Director of the American Academy in Rome. He is Dean Emeritus of the Berkeley Divinity School at Yale University, and he served as a Consultant to the Lambeth Conference of 1998. He has written extensively on the historical background to the relations of the Episcopal Church to the Anglican Communion and on Anglicanism in the nineteenth century. His publications include *Nineteenth-Century Churches: The History of a New Catholicism in Wurttemberg, England, and France* (1987) and *Anglican Orders: Essays on the Centenary of Apostolicae Curae, 1896-1996* (1996).

Andrew Goddard is tutor in Christian Ethics at Wycliffe Hall, Oxford and a member of the Faculty of Theology at Oxford University. He completed a doctorate on the life and work of

Jacques Ellul, and has written widely on political and sexual ethics. Andrew is editor of *Anvil*, the Anglican Evangelical Journal, a Fellow of the Anglican Communion Institute, and a member of the Leadership Team of *Fulcrum: Renewing the Evangelical Centre within the Church of England*. With his wife Elisabeth, he delivered the London Institute for Contemporary Christianity Lectures in 2006 on 'Redeeming Family'.

Paul McPartlan, a Roman Catholic priest of the Archdiocese of Westminster, UK, is Carl J. Peter Professor of Systematic Theology and Ecumenism at The Catholic University of America in Washington DC. He is a member of the International Roman Catholic-Orthodox and Roman Catholic-Methodist theological dialogues, and worked with the International Anglican Roman Catholic Commission for Unity and Mission (IARCCUM) in the production of the Anglican-Roman Catholic text: *Growing Together in Unity and Mission* (2007). A member of the Roman Catholic Church's International Theological Commission, he is author of *The Eucharist Makes the Church: Henri de Lubac and John Zizioulas in Dialogue* (1993, 2006), and many articles on ecclesiology and ecumenism.

Charlotte Methuen is Departmental Lecturer in Ecclesiastical History in the Faculty of Theology at the University of Oxford, specializing in the history of the Reformation. She has taught extensively in Germany. An Anglican priest, she served as Diocesan Director of Training in the Diocese in Europe (2004–05); and currently assists in the Old Catholic parish in Offenbach, Germany. Charlotte is Canon Theologian of the Cathedral and Diocese of Gloucester. She serves on the Church of England's Faith and Order Advisory Group, and is a member of the Meissen Commission and the Anglican

Lutheran International Commission. Her publications include *Kepler's Tübingen: Stimulus to a Theological Mathematics* (Aldershot 1998).

Kenneth Wilson lectured in philosophy and theology at Wesley College and in Bristol University; he was Principal of Westminster College, Oxford from 1981 to 1996 and a member of the Faculty of Theology in the University of Oxford. In 1996 he established the research centre at The Queens Foundation in Birmingham. Kenneth's current research interests are the role of theological enquiry in public debate and ecclesiology. Since 2004 he has been Visiting Fellow of the University of Chichester and Senior Research Fellow of Christ Church University, Canterbury. His publications include *Learning to Hope* (2005). He is a Methodist minister.

Introduction: What's Going on in Anglicanism?

MARK D. CHAPMAN

In this introduction I want to do three things which I hope will place the chapters included in this volume in context. First, I discuss the worldwide character of Anglicanism in relation to post-colonialism and globalization. Secondly, I offer an outline of the immediate circumstances which led to the call for an Anglican Covenant, as well as a brief overview of the implications of the current draft produced in April 2007 (which, because of the timing of the conference, could not be addressed in detail by the rest of the contributors). Finally, I offer some conclusions in terms of reflections on the shape of things to come.

A Global Brand

As I set about writing this introduction, my rather geriatric computer started whirling and gurgling all on its own. A little Microsoft bubble appeared to tell me I had new files to install. At the end of the installation process a box told me that the system was going to check that my software was the real thing – genuine Microsoft Windows. It then told me that it was much better to have Microsoft software than pirated copies, which I am sure is the case. And I am also sure that Microsoft employs lots of people to protect its copyright, and to stop people pilfering its programs and ruining its reputation. Bill Gates is, after all, probably one of the most well-known figures worldwide, and his brand has almost instant recognition, at least among those rich enough to have access to computers (or who aren't that strange breed of dissenters called Apple Mac users).

Anybody who travels across the world will soon realize that in some ways Anglicanism is a bit like Microsoft or any other global brand – in that it covers most of the inhabited world, and is the third largest Christian denomination after Roman Catholicism and Eastern Orthodoxy, with perhaps 80 million members. Rowan Williams, the Archbishop of Canterbury, may not be quite as well known as Bill Gates, but I would guess that his beard and eyebrows command a pretty high degree of international recognition. Anglicanism can be understood as a global brand. Indeed, several recent books have spoken of a 'global Anglicanism'[1] which tends to assume, at least tacitly, that there is something called 'Anglicanism' that transcends national boundaries.

The analogy with multinational companies is not too far-fetched. The story goes something like this and resembles some earlier accounts of missionary history and global expansion of English Christianity.[2] The old missionary societies like the Society for the Propagation of the Gospel and the Church Missionary Society took the English product to the colonies, and eventually made sure there were some local representatives to beat off the competitors and to ensure market saturation. Of course, the product itself had different varieties – for instance, some versions were well finished and rather

---

1   See, for example, Andrew Wingate, Kevin Ward, Carrie Pemberton and Wilson Sitshebo (eds), *Anglicanism: A Global Communion* (New York: Church Publishing Inc., 1998); and most recently, Kevin Ward, *A History of Global Anglicanism* (Cambridge: Cambridge University Press, 2006). See also W. M. Jacob, *The Making of the Anglican Church Worldwide* (London: SPCK, 1997).

2   See, for instance, William L. Sachs, *The Transformation of Anglicanism* (Cambridge: Cambridge University Press, 1993). I outline some of the pitfalls in this approach in my *Anglicanism: A Very Short Introduction* (Oxford: Oxford University Press, 2006), chapter 1. Nevertheless it is also true, for good or ill, that for much of its history, Anglicanism was identical to the global export of different varieties of English Christianity.

colourful (Anglo-Catholicism), while others were a bit less high taste and ornate but had better tunes (Evangelicalism). Quite frequently the local managers could not agree with one another about how best to organize the company in new territories – and very few of them could rely on the traditional state protection which had characterized the mother church.

But, on the whole, nearly all of them were agreed on the value and quality of the good solid English merchandise, and the benefits of English values and an English education. Every now and then the district managers were called back to head office at Lambeth when there were disagreements – sometimes there were anxieties about how to interpret the instructions, or whether the product was being corrupted or distorted by the local conditions. And from the mid-nineteenth century a kind of quality control office for the product gradually developed, which is now devolved to four separate institutions – the so-called Instruments of Unity (the Archbishop of Canterbury (established in 597), the Lambeth Conference (1867), the Anglican Consultative Council (1968), and the Primates' Meeting (1978)).

As in any other global phenomenon, a degree of conflict was hardly surprising. After all, what had worked in the temperate climate of sixteenth-century England might well not be suited for the heat and humidity of the tropics. But, at least among most of elite managers, the stiff upper lip of a good solid English education made sure that disagreements were eventually resolved. For a long time, most of the managers were expatriates. Despite these strong connections with home, however, many of the new churches began to grow and to develop their own ways of doing things – they even started appointing their own indigenous leaders and having their own synods. But something continued to hold them together – perhaps a vague memory of the old country and a fondness for English (and often Victorian) things like *Hymns Ancient and Modern* or robed choirs or churchwardens and archdeacons.

Anglicanism in this sense can be understood as the religious equivalent of cricket.[3]

In the days of the British Empire there was an obvious connection between Anglicanism and England, which was often the source of both religious and political leaders. But as the different churches became self-governing provinces in their own right, so Anglicanism grew to be something far less 'English'. Indeed, there are many connections between the rise of elite education, often organized by the Anglican churches, and the movements towards religious and political independence. The Anglican 'brand', while almost always sharing a large amount with the Church of England, was being adapted to local needs.

There is, however, a crucial difference between cricket and Anglicanism. While cricket retains agreed rules, Anglicanism is far less easy to pin down – to play the game of cricket at an international level all the teams need to sign up to a regulatory framework, and unless they agree there can be no game. But what precisely constitutes the church at an international level is far more difficult to discern. The primary focus of Anglicanism in most parts of the world is unlikely to be on the international institution, as it might be in the more obviously global communion of Roman Catholicism. Instead, Anglicans are more likely to focus on the local, which can be conceived in different ways – for example, the national (or 'provincial') church, the diocese, or even the parish church. The stress on the local means that there is a variety of Anglican 'games' or 'languages' with family resemblances but also with many different nuances in doctrine, style, and practice.

---

3   For example, at the recent Conference of the Clergy of the Diocese of Colombo (Church of Ceylon) in May 2007, at which I spoke on the future of Anglicanism, the daily offices were conducted according to the Book of Common Prayer, hymns were sung from the *English Hymnal*, and the Conference concluded with the inter-deanery cricket competition, won, incidentally, by war-torn Jaffna.

Again the differences with cricket are informative. The International Cricket Council (which changed its name from the Imperial Cricket Conference in 1963) regulates and controls membership as well as rules, and it has the use of various sanctions, including expulsion. In 1970, for instance, the ICC voted that apartheid South Africa should no longer be allowed to be a member. It was reinstated only in 1991 after the change in the political system. The various international regulatory bodies of the Anglican Communion, however, have had no such power – there has traditionally been a moral authority, but this has not been backed up by powers of excommunication and discipline or by any legally constituted authority (although the Archbishop of Canterbury retains the right to excommunicate or not to invite bishops to the Lambeth Conference). The status and function of each of the Instruments of Unity of Anglicanism is open to question. The current crisis perhaps points to the need for something far more like the ICC at the centre of Anglicanism – but it could only work through voluntary participation, which presents, as we shall see, very real problems.

As with cricket, the analogy with multinationals also quickly breaks down. Transnational companies like Nike trainers or Dell computers have shifted production across the globe where the costs are significantly lower. Even what used to be thought of as 'British' companies, like the quality clothes shop, Marks and Spencer, have shifted manufacture away from Britain to developing countries, often offering workers very low wages. Marks and Spencer now imports much of its clothing from North Africa and the Indian sub-continent. While such companies have shifted production across the globe, their head offices in Europe or North America have been careful to retain control over the design and development of the product. Workers have strict guidelines to follow and little autonomy. On the whole, economic control by the multi-nationals keeps power away from workers in developing countries: a decision made in a European boardroom can have instant effects on the other side of the globe. And for global brands, a global market requires a consistent and reliable commodity – for instance, Coca-Cola, which since 1969 has been called 'The Real Thing', needs to be the same brown sugary concoction wherever it is drunk.

Some commentators on globalization, from both left and right, have seen this sort of global saturation by instantly recognized big brands as a symptom of the decline of the now redundant nation state. Susan Strange, for instance, writes that

> the impersonal forces of world markets ... are now more powerful than the states to whom ultimate political authority over society and economy is supposed to belong ... the declining authority of states is reflected in a growing diffusion of authority to other institutions and associations, and to local and regional bodies.[4]

Others have understood the chief problem facing global economics as that of international regulation to mitigate some of the worst excesses of unbridled free trade. Nevertheless, although almost everything in globalization theory is highly contested and requires knowledge in many different disciplines,[5] there are obvious connections between the 'evolving dynamic global structure of enablement and

---

4   Susan Strange, *The Retreat of the State: The Diffusion of Power in the World Economy* (Cambridge: Cambridge University Press, 1994), p. 4. See also Martin Albrow, *The Global Age* (Cambridge: Polity, 1996), p. 85; and Kenichi Ohmae, *The End of the Nation State* (New York: Free Press, 1995), p. 5.

5   On globalization, see David Held, Anthony McGrew, David Goldblatt and Jonathan Perraton, *Global Transformations* (Cambridge: Polity, 1999). See also Hedley Bull, *The Anarchical Society: A Study of Order in World Politics* (London: Macmillan, 1977).

constraint'[6] of globalization, and the diffusion and organization of power and control in a transnational religious organization like Anglicanism.

However, instead of being a singular phenomenon or a unique global brand, Anglicanism, with its huge diversity of contemporary forms, is much more akin to locally produced and – more importantly – locally designed goods aimed primarily at the domestic market. Unlike Coca-Cola or McDonalds, which are much the same everywhere, Anglicanism is made up of a variety of local brands which usually bear similarities with one another – but not always: charismatic exuberance can be unrecognizably different from High Mass. There are no longer any uncontested guidelines or 'product designers' based in any head office outside the primary market. This is, of course, partly a logical development of the founding theology of the Church of England – medieval Christendom, which can be understood as the global phenomenon *par excellence*,[7] mutated into a form of religion completely bounded and under the control of the absolutely sovereign state. At least at the beginning of the Church of England it was impossible for Anglicanism (although the word is anachronistic)[8] to be anything other than a local phenomenon. Although it may be overstating the case a little, given the existence of pan-Protestant alliances, it is not without some justification to see the heart of the Reformation as resting in completely independent, national churches, rather than in much of a conception of an international 'communion'. *Rejection* of an international communion was fundamental to the origin of the English Reformation, even if new models of international communion developed, especially

---

6   Held et al., *Global Transformations*, p. 27.

7   See, for instance, W. H. McNeill, *The Rise of the West: A History of the Human Community* (Chicago: Chicago University Press, 1963).

8   See my *Anglicanism: A Very Short Introduction*, pp. 4–5.

in northern Europe, exemplified, for instance, by the Synod of Dort of 1618–19.[9]

In the days of imperial expansion, the English national church was conceived as something that could be exported as part of the British package: mission was conceived as a one-way process from the centre to the periphery, even if there was always a degree of mutation and modification from the very beginnings. But as the churches took root so they began to take on that aspect of the English church polity which could serve, perhaps ironically, to make them quite unEnglish. They soon began to cultivate their own ecclesiastical independence.[10] Separated from the British Crown, they developed their own self-governing institutions and eventually adopted their own canons and jurisdictional independence from the English church (or occasionally other 'planting' churches like the American Episcopal Church). Consequently, where globalization theorists have spoken of the collapse of national sovereignty, historians of Anglicanism have located its distinctiveness in quite the opposite tendency. Anglicanism has tended to display something of the triumph of national sovereignty and provincial autonomy, sometimes with little

---

9   On this, see Anthony Milton, *Catholic and Reformed: the Roman and Protestant Churches in English Protestant Thought, 1600-1640* (Cambridge: Cambridge University Press, 1995); and *The British Delegation and the Synod of Dort (1618-19)* (Woodbridge: Boydell, 2005). The most popular models for communion among the churches of the Reformation were those based on shared doctrinal confessions, often produced in times of religious or military conflict (like, for instance, the Smalcaldic articles of 1537). The Church of England's relationship to confessions and continental protestantism is both complex and ambiguous. See also Patrick Collinson, *The Religion of the Protestants: The Church in English Society, 1559-1625* (Oxford: Clarendon Press, 1982); and Nigel Voak, *Richard Hooker and Reformed Theology* (Oxford: Clarendon Press, 2003). See also my chapter in this volume.

10   See my *Anglicanism: A Very Short Introduction*, chapter 6.

sense of the need for international regulation or mutual interaction.[11] 'Mature' churches have been understood as those which can survive on their own without the need for assistance.

This understanding of 'provincial autonomy' is further complicated when the traditional 'centre' of Anglicanism (most obviously embodied in the Archbishop of Canterbury, and the inevitable connection with the English Crown, which still appoints him) is identified with the ambiguous historical legacy of the colonial church. Indeed, the very idea of a 'global' church raises enormous questions of power and authority. In the post-colonial world, where is the centre of global power?[12] There is a complex combination of issues stemming from post-colonialism and anti-globalization, which can be detected in some of the recent Anglican squabbles. And it would not be without some justification to suggest that the antagonism towards the American Church by many of the growing churches in the Global South, as well as some critics from within,[13] has at least some of its origins in a post-colonial reaction to what is often understood to be the economic and social imperialism of American liberal values.[14]

---

11 It was not until the 1960s under the influence of Stephen Bayne that formal structures for 'mutual responsibility and interdependence' developed in the Anglican Communion.

12 On this, see Ian T. Douglas and Kwok Pui-Lan (eds), *Beyond Colonial Anglicanism* (New York: Church Publishing Inc., 2001); and Ward, *Global Anglicanism*, chapter 15.

13 The most comprehensive polemical attack on the American church is offered by Ephraim Radner and Philip Turner, *The Fate of Communion: The Agony of Anglicanism and the Future of a Global Church* (Grand Rapids: Eerdmans, 2006).

14 See, for instance, the letter from nine conservative bishops and archbishops written shortly before the 1998 Lambeth Conference: 'Nine senior bishops call for end to ordinations of practising homosexuals', Anglican Communion News Service (ACNS) at: http://www.anglicancommunion.org/acns/lambeth/lc083.html

These analogies with multi-national corporations and cricket, as well as the brief survey of colonial history and globalization, help clarify the questions faced by the Anglican Communion as it seeks to steer a path through the current divisions between and within the different 'provinces' of the Anglican Communion (or, from another point of view, the independent national churches). These questions can be grouped under several points.

1. Can Anglicanism be considered a 'global brand' with a shared identity and set of teachings? Is there anything that can legitimately be called a 'centre' or 'nature' of Anglicanism? Or is it no more a set of family resemblances ultimately dependent on the contingencies of imperial and colonial history? If that is the case, then is the term 'Anglican' any longer usable?

2. Where do we look for markers of Anglican identity? Are they distinctively 'Anglican' or are they shared with other churches? How does one set about defining the limits of diversity (for instance, through the use of Scripture and Creeds in the context of the praying community)?

3. Which leaders and institutions are responsible for defining these limits, boundaries, and characteristics and determining the legitimacy of the theological and ecclesiological methods at work?

4. What – and this is perhaps the most important question – is the relationship between the Instruments of Unity at an international level and the rights and autonomy of the national churches? Who is to decide on how much coercive power is to be given to the 'centre' and how this is implemented in the local churches? How far does this need to be accompanied by changes in canon law to ensure conformity and mutual restraint throughout the Communion?

5. What sort of 'quality control office' (perhaps akin to a more modest version of the Congregation for the Doctrine of the Faith of the Roman Catholic Church) is necessary to ensure

that all the constituent churches are offering the 'real thing', rather than a pale and distorted reflection? What sort of sanctions are necessary in order for this institution to be effective?

The Move Towards an Anglican Covenant

The crisis which has engendered intense debate and division within the Anglican Communion has been provoked principally by the question of homosexuality and its compatibility with the Christian faith. Several key events have highlighted the questions of unity and diversity outlined above. I do not intend to tell the whole story of the debates about homosexuality (which I have discussed elsewhere),[15] but instead I want to raise the ecclesiological and political issues about the nature of the Anglican Communion and what sort of models it has adopted as it seeks to move towards a resolution of its conflicts. What is perhaps most important to stress from the outset is that the divisions are as much *within* as *between* provinces. Thus, while significant portions of American society have come to accept the legitimacy of homosexual relations even among Christians (which is reflected in the majority opinion of the Episcopal Church), many other Americans – including many loyal Episcopalians – find such an approach completely at odds with what they regard as Biblical morality. In some ways what is being played out across the Anglican Communion is a reflection, or even

---

15 See my *Anglicanism: A Very Short Introduction*, pp. 138–43. In his chapter in this volume Andrew Goddard offers a comprehensive account of the various stages of the debate from Lambeth 1998. The most useful set of texts from the American Church (formerly ECUSA and now The Episcopal Church) was published as an appendix to *To Set Our Hope on Christ: A Response to the Invitation of Windsor Report §135* (New York: The Episcopal Church Center, 2005), pp. 63–130.

globalization, of the divisions of American Society. America is a society divided right down the middle – as both the last presidential and congressional elections have demonstrated. Indeed, homosexuality is often one aspect (although this is not always true in the Episcopal Church) of a wider conservative moral agenda that includes hostility to all forms of abortion, support of capital punishment, as well as the strange American constitutional right to carry weapons. It is also part of a theological agenda that tends to locate moral authority in a particular and usually relatively literalist reading of Scripture coupled with a resistance to the influence of culture on theology and what it sees as a diminution of creedal truth.[16]

Although the question of homosexuality found its way onto the agenda at the Lambeth Conferences of 1978 and 1988, the issue did not provoke serious disagreement. Both Conferences affirmed 'heterosexuality as the scriptural norm', but also recognized the need to 'take seriously both the teaching of Scripture and the results of scientific and medical research'.[17] However, the issue of homosexuality led to deep division at the Lambeth Conference of 1998. The initial papers had suggested that the time was not yet ripe for a full discussion or decision about homosexuality – in the same way that the first Lambeth Conference deliberately avoided the divisive issue of Bishop Colenso in 1867,[18] so in 1998 it was recognized by many that any decision over homosexuality would be too divisive. For the first two weeks of the Conference about sixty

---

16 This is particularly obvious in many of the bitter asides in Radner and Turner, *The Fate of Anglicanism*. See, for example, p. 125, n. 21, which sees the use of gender neutral language with reference to the Trinity as 'the most serious issue in respect to ecclesial integrity and tolerable diversity that faces the Anglican Communion'.

17 Lambeth 1978, Resolution 10.3. This was reaffirmed at 1988 (Resolution 34). Details for this section are taken from ACNS at: http://www.anglicancommunion.org/acns/

18 On this, see Alan M. G. Stephenson, *The First Lambeth Conference: 1867* (London: SPCK, 1967).

bishops from across the theological spectrum signed up to discuss questions on human sexuality and to draft a resolution. The sessions were chaired by the Archbishop of Cape Town, Njongonkulu Ndungane, who has recently spoken about these tense discussions:

> We devoted 800 bishop hours to this thorny subject. It was the most difficult group of the whole conference – there was huge pain and division as discussions began. But 800 bishop hours later, we had thrashed out a common position.[19]

The result was an impressive compromise. The bishops wanted to assure homosexuals that 'they are loved by God and that all baptized, believing and faithful persons, regardless of sexual orientation, are full members of the Body of Christ'. While unequivocally opposing sexual abuse as well as promiscuity and adultery, they nevertheless confessed 'that we are not of one mind about homosexuality'. They pointed to four different ways of understanding homosexuality: first, there were those who thought it was simply a disorder which should be changed through God's Grace. Secondly, there were those who thought homosexual activity was straightforwardly against the clear teaching of the Bible and the Church, and was therefore a barrier to the Kingdom of God. Third were those who thought that, while less than ideal, homosexual relationships should be tolerated and preferred to anonymous sexual activity. Finally, there were those 'who believe that the Church should accept and support or bless monogamous covenant relationships between homosexual people and that they may be ordained'. The majority of bishops, the report concluded, were opposed to blessings of homosexual

---

19 Speech to the South African Bishops' Forum, 15 May 2007 at: http://www.anglicancommunion.org/acns/articles/42/75/ acns4284.cfm

partnerships and ordination of practising homosexuals, and many felt that there should be a moratorium. Finally, they wrote:

> We have prayed, studied and discussed these issues, and we are unable to reach a common mind on the scriptural, theological, historical, and scientific questions that are raised. There is much that we do not yet understand. We request the Primates and the Anglican Consultative Council to establish a means of monitoring work done in the Communion on these issues and to share statements and resources among us. The challenge to our Church is to maintain its unity while we seek, under the guidance of the Holy Spirit, to discern the way of Christ for the world today with respect to human sexuality. To do so will require sacrifice, trust, and charity towards one another, remembering that ultimately the identity of each person is defined in Christ.
>
> … Our sexual affections can no more define who we are than can our class, race or nationality. At the deepest ontological level, therefore, there is no such thing as 'an homosexual' or 'an heterosexual'; there are human beings, male and female, called to redeemed humanity in Christ, endowed with a complex variety of emotional potentialities and threatened by a complex variety of forms of alienation.

This statement raises crucial issues about the cultural specificity of homosexuality as a concept and an identity, which continue to be of central importance and in need of further clarification.

Nevertheless things changed very quickly in the course of the 1998 debate. A large number of bishops, especially – but not exclusively – from the Global South, were concerned about whether some of these four options were even open to debate. Many built on the Kuala Lumpur meeting of the 'Anglican Encounter in the South' which was called to reflect on the place of Scripture in the life and mission of the Church. The meeting, which comprised mainly Bishops and Archbishops from the Global South under the leadership of Joseph A. Adetiloye, Archbishop of Nigeria, asserted that ordination of homosexuals was 'totally unacceptable' and was a challenge to the supreme authority of Scripture: 'As provinces and dioceses we need to learn how to seek each other's counsel and wisdom in a spirit of true unity, and to reach a common mind before embarking on radical changes to Church discipline and moral teaching.'[20]

George Carey, the Archbishop of Canterbury, according to the Archbishop of Cape Town,

> found himself under considerable pressure for there to be a fuller resolution on homosexuality. Contrary to all the usual normal procedures for handling resolutions, a draft was presented, and then debated and substantially amended in an hour-and-a-half plenary meeting, of over 600 bishops, spouses, observers, guests, and all in the full glare of the cameras.

What emerged from the debate, which was chaired by Robin Eames, Archbishop of Armagh and which over-ran, was a significantly amended resolution which made it much tougher and less ambiguous than the draft. There was overwhelming support for the final resolution with 526 in favour, 70 against, and 45 abstentions. The final amended text is as follows (italics indicate amendments):

---

20 For the statement see:
   http://www.acahome.org/submenu/docs/kuala.htm

This Conference:

a) commends to the Church the subsection report on human sexuality;

b) in view of the teaching of Scripture, upholds faithfulness in marriage between a man and a woman in lifelong union, and believes that *abstinence [A28]* is right for those who are not called to marriage;

c) recognizes that there are among us persons who experience themselves as having a homosexual orientation. Many of these are members of the Church and are seeking the pastoral care, moral direction of the Church, and God's transforming power for the living of their lives and the ordering of relationships, *and we commit ourselves to listen to the experience of homosexual people. [A24]* We wish to assure them that they are loved by God and that all baptized, believing and faithful persons, regardless of sexual orientation, are full members of the Body of Christ;

d) *while rejecting homosexual practice as incompatible with Scripture, [A36]* calls on all our people to minister pastorally and sensitively to all irrespective of sexual orientation and to condemn *irrational fear of homosexuals [A27]*, violence within marriage and any trivialization and commercialization of sex;

(e) cannot advise the legitimizing or blessing *of same-sex-unions, nor the ordination of those involved in such unions*;

f) requests the Primates and the ACC to establish a means of monitoring the work done on the subject of human sexuality in the Communion and to share statements and resources among us;

g) *notes the significance of the Kuala Lumpur Statement and the concerns expressed in resolutions IV.26, V.1, V.10, V.23, and V.35 on the authority of Scripture in matters of marriage and sexuality and asks the Primates and the ACC to include them in their monitoring process. [A15]*

Section (d) was the most far-reaching. If one accepts the authoritative voice of the Bishops, then the short amended sub-clause which regards 'homosexual practice as incompatible with Scripture' rules out the legitimacy of all forms of homosexual practice, at least for all those Anglicans who regard Scripture as the basis for moral norms, which is one of the most undisputed principles of Anglican method. Lambeth 1998 reaffirmed 'in agreement with the Lambeth Quadrilateral, and in solidarity with the Lambeth Conference of 1888', that 'Holy Scriptures contain "all things necessary to salvation" and are for us the "rule and ultimate standard" of faith and practice.' While other Lambeth Conferences had issued resolutions, advice, and commitments, this particular clause was more far-reaching: the overwhelming majority of the bishops in the Anglican Communion had ruled that something was incompatible with Scripture. This appears to have been done only twice before, once on a sexual matter, with Resolution 19 from 1930 noting that 'illicit and irregular unions are wrong and contrary to the revealed will of God', and once on the illegitimacy of racism and tribalism (1978, Resolution 3).

Possibly because of this Scriptural underpinning, Resolution 1.10 was treated very differently from Lambeth Resolutions of the past. In many quarters it was regarded as a magisterial teaching of the Anglican Communion, and yet what was left unclarified was the precise status of the resolutions of the Lambeth Conference and how far the bishops could claim such an authority. Hitherto it had not claimed to speak with a magisterial voice, but merely offered the combined weight of bishops' moral authority. The Lambeth Conference had always claimed to be nothing more than advisory, and its rulings were always open to future change (as happened, for instance, on polygamy and contraception).[21] But Resolution 1.10 was not treated in this way – instead it was elevated into something like a test of soundness or orthodoxy. Homosexuality was and always would be contrary to Scripture.

Intra-Communion matters were changed decisively in 2003, when the Diocese of New Hampshire elected Gene Robinson, a divorcee in a same-sex relationship, as bishop. His election was confirmed at a meeting of the General Convention in Minneapolis the following August, which some saw as marking the decision by the Episcopal Church to become another denomination and 'to find its primary identity as a liberal but liturgical option within the spectrum of Protestant denominations that make up America's religious kaleidoscope'.[22] The bishops confirmed Robinson's election by 62 to 43 on the basis of a theological report that affirmed that it was 'the responsibility of Dioceses to discern and raise up fit persons for the ministry of word and sacrament to build up the body of Christ in that place'.[23] Again this points to the importance of context – just as the different states in the USA are proud of their independence and resist interference from Washington, so in the American Church there is a similar democratic tradition and resistance to outside interference. The unilateral action of the election of a practising homosexual as a bishop had become primarily a diocesan, rather than a provincial or international matter: the impact on the Anglican Communion was not considered as important as the right of the diocese to act as it saw fit (and which many, including

---

21 See my *Bishops, Saints, and Politics* (London: T & T Clark, 2007), chapter 3.

22 Radner and Turner, *The Fate of Anglicanism*, p. 15.

23 House of Bishops of the Episcopal Church (USA), *The Gift of Sexuality: A Theological Perspective* (March 2003), §7.1.

Robinson himself, regarded as 'prophetic').[24] The old political doctrine of 'states' rights' had apparently won against a 'federal' Anglicanism.

In May 2003, shortly after Robinson's election, matters were complicated still further when the Canadian Diocese of New Westminster authorized rites for same-sex blessings. In England, the Bishop of Oxford nominated Jeffrey John, an openly homosexual priest, although not practising, as suffragan Bishop of Reading. This meant that the new Archbishop of Canterbury, Rowan Williams, was immediately faced with a crisis: very quickly, John, a long-standing friend of Williams (and with him one of the founders of *Affirming Catholicism*) was forced to stand down. At the same time, some provinces were threatening to excommunicate the American and Canadian churches. A number of bishops from Africa and Asia began to intervene in other churches across the Atlantic. This meant that there was an urgent need to examine the nature of relationships between the provinces.

The Archbishop of Canterbury summoned the Primates to an emergency meeting at Lambeth in October 2003. They reaffirmed Resolution 1.10, including the need to listen to homosexuals and to one another, but also noted that the Diocese of New Westminster and the Episcopal Church had acted before the Communion was of one mind:

> as a body we deeply regret the actions of the Diocese of New Westminster and the Episcopal Church (USA) which appear to a number of provinces to have short-circuited that process, and could be perceived to alter unilaterally the teaching of the Anglican Communion on this issue. They do not. Whilst we recognise the juridical autonomy of each province in our Communion, the mutual interdependence of the

---

24 See Gene Robinson's open letter of 24 June 2006, available at: http://www.thewitness.org/article.php?id=1100

provinces means that none has authority unilaterally to substitute an alternative teaching as if it were the teaching of the entire Anglican Communion.

To this extent, therefore, we must make clear that recent actions in New Westminster and in the Episcopal Church (USA) do not express the mind of our Communion as a whole, and these decisions jeopardise our sacramental fellowship with each other. We have a particular concern for those who in all conscience feel bound to dissent from the teaching and practice of their province in such matters. Whilst we reaffirm the teaching of successive Lambeth Conferences that bishops must respect the autonomy and territorial integrity of dioceses and provinces other than their own, we call on the provinces concerned to make adequate provision for episcopal oversight of dissenting minorities within their own area of pastoral care in consultation with the Archbishop of Canterbury on behalf of the Primates.

At Lambeth 1998 (and coming out of the earlier *Virginia Report* on inter-Anglican relations),[25] there had been a suggestion that the Archbishop of Canterbury establish a Commission to consider his role in conflict-resolution. The issues now seemed broader, which led to the setting-up of a commission whose remit included

> urgent and deep theological and legal reflection on the way in which the dangers we have identified at this meeting will have to be addressed. We request that

---

25   Inter-Anglican Theological and Doctrinal Commission, *The Virginia Report: the Report of the Inter-Anglican Theological and Doctrinal Commission* (included in James M. Rosenthal and Nicola Currie (eds), *Being Anglican in the Third Millennium* (Harrisburg PA: Morehouse, 1997), pp. 211–81.

such a commission complete its work, at least in relation to the issues raised at this meeting, within twelve months.[26]

The Lambeth Commission on Communion, which was chaired by Robin Eames, produced *The Windsor Report* in October 2004.[27] It is a lengthy document which seeks to clarify the nature of communion and authority in the Anglican Communion, especially the constraints, restraints and discipline necessary to ensure that the greatest degree of communion between provinces can be maintained. It called for 'Communion-wide dimensions of theological discourse' (§41) and for formal mechanisms to promote inter-provincial conversation and consultation. At the same time, it concluded that the Diocese of New Westminster, the General Synod of the Anglican Church of Canada, and the Episcopal Church had 'acted in ways incompatible with the Communion principle of interdependence, and our fellowship together has suffered immensely as a result of these developments' (§121). Where the *Virginia Report* was virtually silent about sanctions, *The Windsor Report* noted there had to be some legal recognition of the rights of other provinces to constrain unilateral action if there was to be a future for the Communion (§§113–20).

The report has significant flaws, which is hardly surprising given the speed of its production (and the absence of any historian on the Commission). It tends to rely on statements from the Anglican Instruments of Unity as if they are some kind of statute law. This means that they gain the status of

---

26 Primates' Statement, 16 October 2003 at:
    http://www.anglicancommunion.org/acns/articles/36/25/
    acns3633.html

27 The Lambeth Commission on Communion, *The Windsor Report* (London: Anglican Communion Office, 2004). Throughout this book it is abbreviated *TWR*.

magisterial pronouncements and thereby become authoritative, despite the fact that their status has always been questionable and has never been regarded as authoritative where churches do not wish to accept them as such (which is part of what has created the problem in the first place). Historically, authority in Anglicanism has had to be earned rather than pre-supposed: where there is no God-given sovereign power, authority has to be negotiated.

Nevertheless, the Report suggested that one way forward would be the adoption by the churches of the Communion of what it called a 'common Anglican Covenant' which would 'make explicit and forceful the loyalty and bonds of affection which govern the relationships between the churches of the Communion', which would require some form of canon law to ensure its effectiveness (§118). A provisional and fairly lengthy draft was drawn up in Appendix Two. It affirmed the basic principles of the Chicago-Lambeth Quadrilateral,[28] together with some ideas about the requirements for forms of restraint ('mutual reciprocity and forbearance')[29] and responsibilities to one another. This was to be policed by what was called a 'Council of Advice', acting as an extension of the office of the Archbishop of Canterbury.[30] There were huge numbers of responses to *The Windsor Report*, with about two-thirds accepting the idea of a Covenant in some form.[31]

The recommendations of *The Windsor Report* were broadly endorsed by the 2005 Primates' meeting in Dromantine, Northern Ireland,[32] which also requested that the offending

---

28 On this, see below, chapter 4.

29 *TWR* App. 2, Art. 4.

30 *TWR* App. 2, Art. 6.

31 On this see Ian T. Douglas and Paul F. M. Zahl, *Understanding the Windsor Report: Two Leaders in the American Church Speak Across the Divide* (New York: Church Publishing, 2005).

32 For a summary of the Primates' meeting and the work of the Reception Reference Group, see:

churches should voluntarily withdraw from the ACC, which met, without North American representation, at Nottingham in the summer. It endorsed the principles of *The Windsor Report*, as well as planning the 'listening process', which had been part of the original 1998 Resolution. A timetable and a preliminary discussion of the issues involved in producing a Covenant was published in March 2006.[33]

Tension remained high. That summer the Council of Anglican Provinces of Africa (CAPA) issued a statement (*The Road to Lambeth*)[34] that they would 'definitely not attend any Lambeth Conference to which the violators of the Lambeth Resolution are also invited as participants or observers' (although this was not unanimously received). At the meeting of the Primates in Dar-Es-Salaam in February 2007, eight primates refused to receive communion at a service at which Katherine Jefferts-Schori, the recently elected Presiding Bishop of The Episcopal Church, was present. Despite such conflict, however, the Primates managed to reach a common statement which asked the House of Bishops of the Episcopal Church, 'through the Presiding Bishop', to make 'an unequivocal common covenant' not to authorize any rites for same-sex blessings. It concluded with a less than veiled threat:

> If the reassurances requested of the House of Bishops cannot in good conscience be given, the relationship between The Episcopal Church and the Anglican Communion remains damaged at best, and this has

---

http://www.anglicancommunion.org/commission/reception/rep ort/index.cfm.

33 Joint Standing Committee, *Towards an Anglican Covenant: A Consultation Paper on the Covenant Proposal of the Windsor Report* (March 2006).

34 Available at: http://www.globalsouthanglican.org/index.php/comments/ the_road_to_lambeth_presented_at_capa/.

consequences for the full participation of the Church
in the life of the Communion.

At the same time, the Primates discussed the increasing levels
of cross-provincial activity, and made tentative moves towards
provision of 'extended episcopal ministry' for disaffected
parishes in the USA, but under the final invitation of the
Presiding Bishop.

Responses were predictable, with offence being taken by
supporters of both sides of the argument – some were anxious
about the increase of authority being given to the 37 men and
one woman, and many Americans thought there was a failure
to understand the democratic polity of the American Church.
In America and Canada there was little sign of any slowing in
the process of moving towards rites for same-sex blessings.
After some hesitation, the Archbishop of Canterbury
eventually agreed to meet with the American bishops in
September 2007. In May 2007, Peter Akinola, Primate of All
Nigeria, installed Martyn Minns as a bishop for a branch of the
Nigerian church in the USA (CANA). In May 2007 the
invitations to the Lambeth Conference were published –
invitations were not sent to Gene Robinson, nor to Minns, nor
to the eight American bishops of the Anglican Mission in
America of the Church of Rwanda.[35] The Nigerian Church
responded by saying that this was tantamount to withholding
the invitation from all Nigerian bishops, and shortly afterwards
the Archbishop of Uganda, Henry Orombi, wrote:

> We note that all the American Bishops who consented
> to, participated in, and have continued to support the
> consecration as bishop of a man living in a

---

35 On the relationships between African churches and dissident
congregations in the United States, see Miranda K. Hassett, *Anglican
Communion in Crisis: How Episcopal Dissidents and Their African Allies
are Reshaping Anglicanism* (Princeton: Princeton University Press,
2007).

homosexual relationship have been invited to the
Lambeth Conference. These are Bishops who have
violated the Lambeth Resolution 1.10, which rejects
'homosexual practice as incompatible with Scripture'
… Accordingly, the House of Bishops of the Church of
Uganda stands by its resolve to uphold the *Road to
Lambeth*.

What will happen at the Lambeth Conference in 2008, and
precisely who will turn up, is, of course, an open question, but
what is certain is that the Conference will be crucial for the
future of the Anglican Communion. It is reassuring to know
that it will begin in retreat, Bible study, and prayer.

The Primates in Tanzania were also able to consider a first
draft of a Covenant which had been written with remarkable
efficiency at the first meeting of the Covenant Design Group in
the Bahamas in January 2007.[36] It is a more developed version
than that included in *The Windsor Report*, and is more
historically aware about the nature and development of
Anglicanism. What is most significant is that the first use of
the word 'covenant' is as a verb (§1). The model of covenant
used is far closer to the agreements between churches in
ecumenical discussion than to any Biblical model[37] – it may
even have been better to avoid a word which has such a
complex and contested religious history. As used in this draft it
means much the same as 'pledge' or 'agree to abide by'. This
sense of commitment is the key point of the document – it
amounts to a voluntary pledge by the individual churches,
firstly, to a set of definitions about the nature of Anglicanism,

---

36 A slightly modified version was issued in April 2007: Anglican
    Communion Office, *An Anglican Covenant: A Draft for Discussion*
    (April 2007), available at:
    http://www.anglicancommunion.org/commission/d_covenant/
    docs/Draft%20Covenant%20Text%20070504.pdf

37 See below, chapter 9.

and, secondly, and more crucially, to a method for solving disputes.

First, then, it seeks to understand Anglicanism broadly along the lines of the Chicago-Lambeth Quadrilateral, but with a stronger emphasis on the Reformation formularies and the importance of mission (§2). It goes on to stress the need for communion and interdependence, both in terms of the common mission to the world and the importance of learning from one another. The catholic and apostolic faith is understood as a shared inheritance (§§3, 4). While some may quibble at the explicit emphasis on the 'rich history of the Church in Britain and Ireland', the statements are clear, concise and very different from any form of confession. Importantly, too, there is an emphasis on reading Scripture respectfully in the light of scholarship and under the authority of bishops and synods (§3.3).

The draft then goes on to discuss the structures to which the member churches would covenant themselves. It reaffirms the historic episcopate (§5.1) and the four 'Instruments of Communion' (§5.2). However, what is conspicuously lacking in this section is any mention of synodality. It emphasizes one important aspect of the Anglican churches – 'the historic episcopate locally adapted' – without noting that in all provinces bishops act only in relation to synods. It may indeed be wrong to see the Lambeth Quadrilateral as the final word on Anglican polity. Even in the Church of England, which was relatively late in embracing formal synodical structures, from the very beginning Parliament was sovereign over the church, and the crown was (and still in theory is) responsible for the appointment of bishops. Some formal acknowledgement of the interdependence of the episcopate on synods seems imperative if the Anglican Communion is not to become an episcopally dominated and unrepresentative church (and here, I think, the American criticisms have some substance). The Instruments of Communion might need to be significantly modified better to reflect synodality before member churches will commit themselves to any covenant.

The draft Covenant concludes with what is probably its most important section: 'The Unity of the Communion' (§6). The churches will pledge themselves to 'have regard for the common good of the Communion'. The draft wisely encourages open discussion, listening and perpetual testing, and warns against foreclosure of debate (which may mean that Resolution 1.10 will need to be modified). It then moves towards an injunction that those who covenant themselves will

> heed the counsel of our Instruments of Communion in matters which threaten the unity of the Communion and the effectiveness of our mission. While the Instruments of Communion have no juridical or executive authority in our Provinces, we recognise them as those bodies by which our common life in Christ is articulated and sustained, and which therefore carry a moral authority which commands our respect (§6.4).

This resists the temptation to create a new Anglican Communion canon law (although it may well be the case that provinces will incorporate the Covenant into their canons). The Covenant thus recognizes that acceptance of the counsels of the Communion structures rests on the voluntary commitment of member churches. Where matters cannot be resolved by 'mutual admonition and counsel', then the Covenant proposes that matters are submitted to the Primates' Meeting (§6.5.1), who may ask for further guidance from the other Instruments of Unity (§6.5.2), and will then offer 'guidance and direction' (§6.5.3).

Where the member churches refuse to heed the guidance, there can be no 'legal' sanctions (since these have been ruled out). This means that ultimately the one sanction that remains is expulsion from the Instruments of Unity and thus the Communion altogether, which would presumably be the decision of the Primates:

> We acknowledge that in the most extreme circumstances, where member churches choose not to fulfil the substance of the covenant as understood by the Councils of the Instruments of Communion, we will consider that such churches will have relinquished for themselves the force and meaning of the covenant's purpose, and a process of restoration and renewal will be required to re-establish their covenant relationship with other member churches (§6.6).

A voluntary commitment by member churches to abide by a decision of what amounts to an understanding of international catholic order and structure, upon which the Covenant is founded, appears to be sensible if the Anglican Communion is to withstand the contemporary conflicts. Nevertheless the proposed solution seems untenable – while relatively cheap and easily convened, the Primates' Meeting, which is rather like the US Senate in giving equal representation to all provinces regardless of size, is unlikely to command the respect necessary for a Covenant to succeed. Given the disparity of sizes of churches and the quite different systems of accountability, appointment and perceptions of primacy, the emphasis on the Primates' Meeting does not seem to me to be a very sensible way forward, and downplays the importance of synods. There is, after all, little point in creating a structure that few would pledge themselves to abide by. Besides, there is something disingenuous about giving more power to determine communion and decide what constitutes the 'common mind' of the Communion to a group who do not even know how to share sacramental communion with one another.

It may well turn out that none of the current Instruments of Unity is capable of commanding sufficient authority across the churches. Consequently, what the drafting group should focus on is creating some form of Anglican Representative Council which would command respect and to which member churches would be content to delegate their sovereignty. Otherwise it is hard to imagine the Covenant becoming a workable agreement. If anything is to work, there will also need to be a huge effort to create a consultative system that promotes dialogue and conversation in a more open and engaged manner – ecclesiastical politicians like Primates may not be best at conducting this sort of business, and more weight might need to be directed towards the educational structures of the Communion in promoting scholarship and free enquiry.[38] One should never underestimate the importance of power in ecclesiastical history. As E. H. Carr wrote about international relations between the wars: 'International order and "international solidarity" will always be slogans of those who feel strong enough to impose them on others.'[39] The odds may be stacked against the Covenant, but some sort of extra-provincial body seems necessary to retain the bonds of affection and inter-dependence required in any church that can claim to be catholic – but it is important to get it right before embarking on a course that could be counter-productive and create yet more schism.[40]

---

38 See especially the promising work of the group *Theological Education for the Anglican Communion* which reported to the February 2007 Primates' Meeting. In May 2007 it produced a brief document, *The Anglican Way: Signposts on a Common Journey*, which speaks of the need to 'follow the Lord with renewed humility'. This is available at: http://www.anglicancommunion.org/acns/articles/42/75/acns4289.cfm

39 E. H. Carr, *The Twenty Years Crisis, 1919-1939* (London: Papermac, 1981), p. 87.

40 While I would not agree with their diagnosis nor adopt their rhetoric, the conciliar solution proposed by Radner and Turner

Conclusion

All this shows that there are shifts and realignments going on in the Anglican Communion – as I suggested in my opening section, much of this is connected with a reaction to what is perceived as liberal imperialism, and it fits neatly into a post-colonial understanding.[41] There are frequent references in the literature of the conservatives in North America and England to the decline of the liberal churches and the exponential growth of the churches in the developing countries, especially in Africa, as well as conservative churches at home. One Nigerian bishop has spoken of the American church being like an unruly child that needs disciplining – which tidily reverses the direction of mission, which was so often about the project of civilization, or what Samuel Wilberforce, champion of the Colonial Bishoprics' Fund, once called training 'mankind in the habits of truth, morality and justice, instead of leaving them in the imbecility of falsehood and perpetual childhood'.[42]

But what remains unclear is precisely why it is that homosexuality should have become such an important and divisive subject, especially in parts of Africa. As Kevin Ward points out, it may have something to do with making a stand against what seem to be the inexorable forces of modernization in which the mainline denominations are often one of the main carriers – ironically, perhaps, rather than being an attack on the Enlightenment, it is a product of a changing understanding of what it is to be human:[43] 'Homophobia', he claims, 'is as much a western intrusion as is homosexual identity'.[44] Perhaps

---

seems to offer a way forward for the Communion (see *The Fate of Communion*, chapters 5 and 6). I have discussed the lessons to be learnt from medieval conciliarism in my chapter later in this volume.

41 Philip Jenkins, *The Next Christendom: The Coming of Global Christianity* (Oxford: Oxford University Press, 2002), p. 2.

42 See my *Anglicanism: A Very Short Introduction*, p. 11.

43 Ward, *A History of Global Anglicanism*, pp. 308–18.

44 Ward, *A History of Global Anglicanism*, p. 310.

the emphasis on homosexuality is really an export of the tensions of the American churches across the globe – and is evidence for a strange form of the globalization of specifically American moral questions:

> The fact that the conflict has focussed so fiercely on homosexuality is itself an indication of the ways in which what is essentially a conflict within western secular society has spilled over to the rest of the world, itself coming to terms with modernity and the increasing dominance of secularity and its discontents.[45]

This is ironic given that the formularies of Anglicanism, especially the Chicago-Lambeth Quadrilateral of 1888, were designed to unite all Christians by an American Church that sought to unite its own society after the bloodshed of the Civil War.[46] Yet that society still remains divided between north and south and conservative and liberal. So one might even ask – is the current crisis at least in part a lingering after-effect of the failure to reconstruct America into one nation after the Civil War?

Ensuring that people talk to one another is crucial, and it is better to do it outside the law court – a Covenant might promote that sort of conversation. But, in my view, nothing is likely to be very successful unless there is some attention paid to the tiny phrase from Resolution 1.10 that regards 'homosexual practice as incompatible with Scripture'. Patently, significant numbers of Anglicans would disagree and would want to see this as a changeable rather than infallible teaching – while most of them would presumably accept that there can be a diversity of opinion, and it would be foolish to deny that the tradition of all the churches has been to condemn

---

45 Ward, *A History of Global Anglicanism*, p. 315.
46 See below, chapter 4.

homosexual practice; for a Covenant to work there needs to be an agreement that it is possible to hold divergent views on this matter and still be counted a loyal Anglican. While 'prophetic' acts like the consecration of an openly homosexual bishop may simply make matters worse, complete foreclosure devalues the listening process and the possibility that even bishops may have got things wrong – simply think of slavery, or even contraception. Some leaders might be counselled to read the *Cloud of Unknowing* or another apophatic text before making such bold judgements.

Unless there can be a diversity of opinion about homosexuality there can be no possibility of a workable Covenant. There is little point in agreeing to a moratorium on further ordinations of practising homosexuals or same-sex blessings if it is impossible even to imagine that change to the 'common mind' of the Anglican Communion might be possible. It is worth reminding the Covenant Drafting Group of Article XXI of the Thirty-nine Articles of Religion ('Of the Authority of General Councils'), which are mentioned in the Draft Covenant as a 'witness to Christian truth' (§2.3): General Councils, 'when they be gathered together, (forasmuch as they be an assembly of men, whereof all be not governed with the Spirit and Word of God,) ... may err, and sometimes have erred, even in things pertaining unto God'. The common mind of Anglicanism needs to be tempered by the humility to acknowledge human fallibility, even among the leaders and decision-makers of the church.

Anglicanism would become much narrower without the majority of Americans and Canadians (and many others) who think that homosexuality is compatible with Scripture. But since Resolution 1.10 has become the test of orthodoxy among significant portions of Anglicanism, there is little chance of this happening (and the exclusion of North Americans from the Anglican Communion may be what many desire). This does not inspire much optimism about the success of the Covenant.

But if that is the case then it might be better for the Anglican Communion to refocus on the huge number of parochial, diocesan and other personal links that enable communication to happen informally in Christian love and charity – and not just with Anglicans. There is no substitute for worshipping, studying, learning, and eating together. Indeed, it may be that companionship is a better way forward than Covenant, and will lead to a far deeper sense of communion.

1

Baby's First Steps
Can the Covenant Proposal Ever Walk?

Gregory K Cameron

There was a moment in May 2003 when the Anglican Communion Office staff came out of a very difficult session of the Primates' Meeting in Gramado in Brazil. 'That was pretty tough going, wasn't it?' I said to a colleague, who replied: 'You haven't seen anything yet; just you wait until after New Hampshire!' At that stage, New Hampshire meant nothing to me except that it was a state where an early primary for the presidential election takes place. 'What's going to happen in New Hampshire?' I asked, and he said 'Well, the bishop they are going to elect is in an open gay relationship.' The rest is history …

That event during the summer changed the face of Anglicanism. The Primates, in May 2003, had taken a decision that they were meeting a little too often and decided that they would extend the gap between Primates Meetings' from one year to two years. They found themselves meeting six months later! At that point, October 2003, the Primates decided that they would appoint the Lambeth Commission on Communion. My initial appointment in the Anglican Communion Office was as Secretary to that Commission, and, although my initial appointment was as Director of Ecumenical Affairs, my work became increasingly less ecumenical affairs, and more in looking after what has been called the Windsor-Lambeth process.

Koinonia Ecclesiology

However, it is important not to forget the ecumenical context. Let us not pretend that the debates going on within Anglicanism are about an Anglican problem. Issues of human sexuality are an ecumenical problem and each church is facing the same tensions, both over the relationship of the local church to the universal, as well as over the ethical issues that are under debate. Many of those churches are looking at how the Anglican Communion is solving its tensions, as mirrors or templates for the way in which they themselves will have to address those questions in due course.

It is the ecumenical world above all others that has developed the *koinonia* theology of the Church, which has been so present in discourse in the Christian world during the twentieth century. Two of the reasons why *koinonia* ecclesiology has become so prominent are because it offers some very distinct insights.

First, it offers an egalitarian model of the Church as opposed to a hierarchical one: 'egalitarian' in the sense that a *koinonia* ecclesiology sees all members of the Church living in relationship with one another, rather than being subject to a particular structure or hierarchy. Secondly, it offers a porous model of the Church rather than one which is strictly demarcated: 'porous' because it allows the whole of the people of God, even across the different denominations, to be drawn together to a greater or lesser degree into the life which is at the core of the Church. Those two aspects of equality and porosity are ones which we need to hold on to very strongly.

There is a third personal reason for me which commends a *koinonia* ecclesiology: it reflects most clearly my own experience of Christian discipleship. It is that sense of encounter with Christ that we discover in another disciple, in another Christian, which is so profoundly important to my own experience of being a disciple. The tremendous experience for me which flowed from being appointed Director of Ecumenical Affairs for the Anglican Communion was that suddenly I was able to meet with the whole *oikumene* of God's Church: I was able to meet with Anglican Christians from the USA, from New Zealand, from Singapore, from South Africa; I was able to meet with Christians from the huge diversity of the Christian families across the globe, from the Oriental Orthodox to the Pentecostals. Indeed, one of the deepest ironies for me is that having been appointed to a post whose brief is to build *koinonia* and to deepen fellowship, I find that my own Communion is beginning to squabble and endanger that *koinonia* we have with one another.

This reminds us that if we adopt a *koinonia* ecclesiology, the biggest criticism that can be offered of it is the failure of the Church to live by it. One significant criticism of *The Windsor Report* is that it is too idealistic in the presentation that it makes of our life together. Simon Golding's book, *Love, Sex & Tragedy: how the ancient world shapes our lives*,[1] has a chapter that looks at the classical history of Christianity with a very sharp gaze, and observes just how violent and quarrelsome early Christianity was. We are apt to forget that. We are apt to idealize the past and see the controversies of the present time as recent expressions of church life, when the truth is that as Christians we have a woeful record of failing to live up to the standards of *koinonia* which is the will of the Lord for the Church.

The Crisis of Anglicanism in the Twenty-first Century

When we come to describe the current crisis, it was Archbishop Rowan Williams who, speaking to the Anglican delegates gathered at the World Council of Churches in Porto

---

1   *Love, Sex & Tragedy: How the Ancient World Shapes our Lives* (London: John Murray, 2004).

Alegre in February 2006, said that the difficulty about the current crisis in the Anglican Communion is that as Anglicans we are failing to recognize the patterns of obedience to Christ in one another;[2] there are patterns of obedience to Christ which are fundamental to Christian discipleship and for some, those patterns are no longer recognizable across the Communion. In the USA or the Global North the pattern of obedience is deeply committed to questions of justice and inclusion, and which can find a pattern of obedience based on literal faithfulness to Scripture just too limiting and too prejudiced. In the Global South the pattern of obedience is based on faithful adherence to Scripture, and there are many who see the discipleship of the churches of the Global North as one which is abandoning the standards of faith by which they live. The real challenge in the twenty-first century for Anglicans is whether we can recover a sense of recognizing those patterns of obedience in each other once more.

Are we committed to learning how Christ is speaking to the different parts of our Church, and allowing Christ to speak to us through them? There are three hallmarks of the life of *koinonia* which need to be commended to the Church today. First of all – humility, which is an attitude of being ready to see Christ at work in the other, rather than just in oneself. Secondly, generosity, which is giving the best interpretation to what others are seeking to articulate, rather than the worst. Thirdly, hospitality, which is ensuring that the Christian community that we build is one in which people feel safe to express what God has laid on their heart, rather than what they think they need to say in order to qualify for membership. Humility, generosity, hospitality – these are fundamental to the experience of *koinonia*. These are fundamental to the

2   See Report of the Assembly of the World Council of Churches held at Porto Alegre, Brazil, 14–23 February 2006.

worship that I experience as an Anglican travelling across the globe. They are fundamental to the success of meetings that try to bring together people of different views. It is only if we can meet in the expectation that we are ready to learn, to listen to what others are going to say to us, where we create a community where people are free to speak their mind, where we are as generous as possible in listening to what others have to say, that we can be successful in our conversations.

One of the fundamental things about *koinonia*, which was one of the fundamental insights of *The Windsor Report*,[3] is that if this is true of the individual level of Christian discipleship, it should be true as well at the level of the way in which one church relates to another. What can be said of the way in which two Christians walk together should be true of the way in which two churches relate to one another as well. When the Lambeth Commission on Communion met, it recognized this as one of the fundamental problems in the life of the Communion today – that there was fundamentally a breakdown of trust, that the churches of the Global South no longer trusted the churches of the North in their discipleship, and that the churches of the North were becoming increasingly distrustful of the agenda and of the Gospel values of the Global South.

Finding a Way Forward

How did the Lambeth Commission on Communion seek to change that? If you ask a group of Christians for the solution to any problem, they tend to put forward a solution which is a mirror of their own discipleship. Say to the Anglican Communion Legal Advisors' Network 'How do we solve the

---

3   *The Windsor Report* (London: The Anglican Communion Office, 2004), esp. §§4–11.

tensions in the Anglican Communion?' and they reply 'What you need is an international code of canon law.' Ask the Inter-Anglican Theological and Doctrinal Commission the same question and they say, as they said in their meeting in September 2006, 'We need an Inter-Anglican Doctrinal Tribunal that will solve the tensions by offering an authoritative doctrinal assessment of any development.' As a canon lawyer myself, I am afraid I find all too appealing the idea of an international body of Anglican canon law.

It was an idea that the Lambeth Commission played with a great deal, to the extent that they commissioned some of the canonists within their membership to develop the shape of what an international code of Anglican canon law might look like. This goes alongside a process that the Anglican Communion Legal Advisors' Network is undertaking at the moment, where they are looking at the existing canon law of the thirty-eight provinces and trying to see in what ways Anglican canon law can be said to cohere. They have found a remarkable coherence. The network has uncovered in the order of 600 principles of canon law which are the same across the thirty-eight different Provincial bodies of canon law. That those patterns of canon law are so similar should give us a certain level of confidence about Anglican integrity and shared identity. When the members of the Lambeth Commission came to discuss it, however, they were profoundly uncertain that such an approach was the right one. The feeling was that it was overly juridical, overly codified and not flexible enough to capture something of the life of the Spirit in the churches. Rather, the Commission turned to the concept of covenant as one which was far more dynamic, and far more rooted in the Christian tradition than ideas of juridical codification. And so the idea of an Anglican Covenant was born in *The Windsor Report* published in October 2004.

The Anglican Covenant

Jewellers assess the quality of a diamond by the four 'C's: by its cut, its carats, its colour and its clarity. I'm not an expert on diamonds but I do want to offer you four 'C's of my own. I will summarize the ideas involved in the proposed Covenant in terms of four words, each beginning with the letter 'c', although three of them are not being proposed for the Anglican Communion.

1. *Contract*

How first of all is the idea of a covenant different from that of a contract? What is being proposed for the Anglican Communion is not a contract. This is where I would want to take issue with the sort of definition which says that a covenant is a solemn agreement to perform an action. A contract is when a person makes a solemn agreement with someone else – 'If you do this, I will do that' or 'I will do this, if you will do that'. It is a bilateral agreement to do something, to enact something, to complete something. Then the contract is completed – finished. When we complete the sale of a house, for example, the end of a contract is to finish a relationship, completing the sale of a house, with the parties going their separate ways. I do not think that what the Communion is asking for is a contract, a binding agreement that churches will perform this, or deliver that.

2. *Confession*

The second 'C' with which to contrast the covenant is a 'Confession'. Christians have already been through that period of history when the Church survived by producing confessions: the Thirty-nine Articles; the Westminster Confession; the Augsburg Confession, and so on. They were very useful and they contributed a great deal to the life of the Church, but the reality is that life in the Church today is far more diverse than it was in the sixteenth century and, on the whole, laity are far better educated than they were in the sixteenth century. The idea that a small group of people could write an exhaustive definition of Christianity to which eighty million Anglicans in all corners of the globe are expected to sign up is almost impossible to conceive. Furthermore, the idea of a confession is difficult because Christians never know what the next doctrinal disagreement is going to be about. We could write the fullest confession we could envisage and tomorrow we will find that someone in the Church is offering some new and radical interpretation which we just had not thought about.

3. *Code*

Finally, the proposal is not an attempt to develop a 'Code'. I have already mentioned the idea of an international Code of Canon Law. I am persuaded that the Anglican Churches would benefit from a clearer understanding of the law which unites them rather than that which divides them. However, the idea of a Code falls prey to many of the ideas expressed in the idea of a confession. It is simply impossible to cope with all the circumstances that arise.

Some time ago the Cameron family went to stay with another family. In the course of the weekend, the families decided that it would be a pleasurable thing to have a game of Monopoly. The Cameron family and the Hardman family played Monopoly. This might appear to have been fairly straightforward but then someone landed on the square marked 'Go'. Someone said that if you land on the square marked 'Go', you get £400, not £200. Someone else, during their first time round the board, wanted to buy Leicester Square. 'You don't start buying property until the second time round the board,' someone objected. It turned out that the Cameron received rules of playing Monopoly were very different to the Hardman received rules of playing Monopoly!

The trouble with a code is that codes change to meet specific circumstances, and specific circumstances vary, particularly in a global communion where 44 churches, or, more accurately, 38 churches and 6 extra-provincial jurisdictions, have very different circumstances to address.

4. *Covenant*

So by proposing a covenant, the proposal is not that the Anglican Communion should adopt a contract, a confession or a code. What then is a covenant about? Other chapters in this collection give very powerful expositions, but at the heart of the idea of covenant is the biblical context in which a covenant is a promise to behave in a certain way, a solemn undertaking by one party to adopt a particular attitude towards another. It is not so much a contract (which is an agreement to deliver a specific action), but rather it is to have regard to a person in a particular way, to behave consistently towards them in a particular manner. It is quintessentially represented by the Covenant between God and the people of Israel – 'I will be your God, and you will be my people.'

This, I think, must be at the heart of any future Anglican Covenant. The two concepts of communion and covenant must be inextricably linked. It is about the way in which the Anglican churches behave with one another: meeting with one another as equals, with hospitality and with generosity, which will enable our Communion to survive and flourish in the twenty-first century.

This chapter is rather flippantly entitled 'Baby's First Steps'! What is meant by that? The baby which I think that we are trying to encourage to mature is the baby of global Anglicanism in which the family of 44 churches can live together. The covenant could be the way to enable that living together to flourish.

The Covenant Process

In terms of formal process, the idea of the covenant was proposed in *The Windsor Report* and accepted by two of the Instruments of Communion at the Primates' Meeting in Dromantine, assuming that the Archbishop of Canterbury gave his assent to the proposal at that point. The thirteenth meeting of the Anglican Consultative Council (ACC-13) at Nottingham also gave its assent, so three Instruments of Communion are now on board. At the meeting of the Joint Standing Committee of the Anglican Consultative Council and the Primates last March the paper *Towards an Anglican Covenant* was adopted. The paper asked for two things, firstly for the establishment of a Covenant Design Group which would carry the work of drafting a covenant forward, and secondly that the paper *Towards an Anglican Covenant* would itself become a consultation paper for discussion and would seek contributions from across the Communion. A number of responses have already been received, for example, the Affirming Catholicism response and the Inclusive Church response. Many other groups and individuals are making responses to that paper. When the Covenant Design Group first met in Nassau, Bahamas in January 2007 under the chairmanship of Archbishop Drexel Gomez, it already saw tabled in the order of 32 papers and contributions to the discussion. More are welcome.

The Design Group will make an interim report to the Primates at their meeting in Tanzania next month. The good news is that the Group made enough progress to be able to give a positive report to them. I very much hope that the Primates will choose to make that interim report part of the process and consultation that goes on in the Communion. We need a process by which all the Communion is drawn into discussion of the covenant.[4]

There is a question about who signs a covenant on behalf of the Provinces of the Anglican Communion. Should it be the ACC as the body which is most synodical within the life of the Communion and the only body which has a constitution for its Communion role, within which, already, is something about the terms of membership of the Communion. Should it be the Lambeth Conference, the gathering of the 850 bishops of the Anglican Communion, since those gathered are the chief pastors of their dioceses and therefore in theory most able to speak on behalf of their dioceses? Indeed, it has been argued that it is the Lambeth Conference which is the most representative body of the Communion since there is at least one person from each diocese present.

Is it the Provinces themselves who have to agree to the covenant? Any covenant that is going to work in the life of the Communion must be one in which each of the churches of the Anglican Communion find themselves described. That is probably the essential point. The covenant will only work if, when people read it, they are able to say 'yes, this is a statement about the church to which I belong and to which I wish to continue to belong'. And this is no mean task.

There is an old a story about a particular Shaker congregation in North America which was riven with argument. The older people and the young people of the congregation were in bitter dispute because it seemed the younger members of the congregation wanted too much riotous dancing in their worship. The older members found this very upsetting. The elders met to try to solve the problem.

---

4   Subsequent to the meeting at which this chapter was originally delivered, the Primates met in Tanzania at the end of February 2007 and authorized such a process.

45

The solution they came up with was this: at future occasions of worship, the older members of the church should sit around the edge of the church, rather than in the centre. The young people should be allowed to dance in the centre. But as they danced around in the centre of the church, whenever they passed the older members they should stop and bow to them, and the older members in turn would bow respectfully to the younger people. That, I believe, sums up the attitude of *koinonia*. That is the behaviour to which we must be committed in an Anglican Covenant.

2

Unity and Diversity, Communion and Covenant: Theological, Ecclesiological, Political and Missional Challenges for Anglicanism

ANDREW GODDARD

The opening section of the Archbishop of Canterbury's crucial reflections on the Anglican Communion is headed 'The Anglican Communion: A Church in Crisis?'[1] In the months since that was published, indeed even since the Affirming Catholicism conference of January 2007, the question mark appears to have been fading rapidly.[2] It is even more clearly the case that, as Archbishop Rowan proceeded to say in his reflections, 'there is no way in which the Anglican Communion can remain unchanged by what is happening at the moment'.[3] What follows is an attempt to accomplish three main goals. Firstly, to offer a brief account of where we are in

---

1   Rowan Williams, 'The Challenge and Hope of Being an Anglican Today: A Reflection for the Bishops, Clergy and Faithful of the Anglican Communion', 27 June 2006.

2   I am grateful to Richard Jenkins, Mark Chapman and others who organized the excellent day conference and invited me to speak. The Church of England and the Anglican Communion as a whole undoubtedly needs more such occasions where there is genuine mutual listening and dialogue between different traditions and outlooks. This chapter is based on the paper given on that day but has been revised in the light of significant developments up to Easter 2007.

3   Rowan Williams, 'Challenge and Hope'.

47

the Communion and why we have got there. Secondly, to examine and critique two common approaches to the question identified by Affirming Catholicism as a central concern in the current crisis – that of unity and diversity within Anglicanism. Thirdly, to propose that in response we need to focus on issues relating to both communion and covenant and we need to do so from four angles – the theological, ecclesiological, political/institutional and, as the context of it all, the missional.

1. Where Are We and How Did We Get Here?

There are many different ways of representing to ourselves the current difficulties within the Communion. Indeed, one of the challenges we face is that there are not only diverse and divergent proposals as to how to proceed but a similar range of interpretations as to where we are and why we are there.[4] One is to reduce it largely – in some cases almost solely – to a matter of political power-play and a struggle for theological dominance. How that is represented then depends on one's own prejudices. For some, it is an attempt by fundamentalists and evangelicals to take over and control the Church of England and wider Communion and to drive out those they see as liberals and bring an end to traditional Anglican toleration and diversity.[5] This political agenda is now viewed

---

4   To my mind the best analysis is that found in Ephraim Radner and Philip Turner's volume of essays, *The Fate of Communion: The Agony of Anglicanism and the Future of a Global Church* (Grand Rapids: Eerdmans, 2006).

5   This reading is that offered by Stephen Bates in his various writings, particularly his *A Church At War: Anglicans and Homosexuality* (London: Hodder & Stoughton, revised edition, 2005).

as powerful because of the newly invigorated and increasingly dominant post-colonial, theologically conservative Global South led by Nigeria.[6] For others, the problem is that the Communion remains too much under the sway (theologically, financially, organizationally) of the old Northern liberal Anglican establishment, led by the imperialistic USA, and we are witnessing a struggle for the soul of Anglicanism and the biblical gospel in the face of the cultural captivity of the declining Western branches of Protestant Christendom and the new life and growth of the younger churches.[7]

Clearly, as always in the Church down through the centuries, issues of politics, power and personalities play an important role and there are probably some elements of truth in both of these accounts and other analyses and diagnoses. However, they are also incomplete and to that extent at times become crude caricatures that distort reality. It cannot be denied that there are also significant matters of faith – fundamental theological, moral and ecclesiological issues – at the heart of our tensions. Here the title of the conference, focusing on unity and diversity within Anglicanism, does a pretty good job at getting to the heart of the problem. Certainly the media's belief – encouraged by some within Anglicanism – that, apart from questions of power, this is all just about sex, is

---

6   The writings of Philip Jenkins, especially his *The Next Christendom: The Coming of Global Christianity* (Oxford: Oxford University Press, 2002, revised edition, 2007) and *The New Faces of Christianity: Believing the Bible in the Global South* (Oxford: Oxford University Press, 2006) are the most influential and among the best guides to this phenomenon.

7   Examples of some form of this perception can be found in writings on various websites such as that of Anglican Mainstream (http://www.anglican-mainstream.net) and Global South Anglican (http://www.globalsouthanglican.org) where Michael Poon's contributions are particularly perceptive in relation to such matters.

seriously flawed. Homosexuality is simply the presenting issue. The more fundamental challenge is the need to articulate – and then embody – a biblical and Anglican vision of how the Church of God maintains and nurtures and expresses its unity while both allowing genuine and legitimate diversity and determining the limits and boundaries of such diversity.

Although this is not exactly a new question it presses in on us now with particular urgency for a number of reasons. Firstly, the growing Global South – particularly African and South East Asian – churches are now better represented within Communion structures. As one of the Global South leaders recently pointed out

> It is, for example, easy to forget that just under thirty years ago at the 1978 Lambeth Conference (the first I attended) there were only 80 bishops present from Africa. That almost doubled over the next decade so there were 175 present in 1988. By 1998, Nigeria alone (which had not even been a separate province in 1978) sent 59 bishops and Kenya 26. That means that in 1998 between them these two provinces sent more bishops than the continent as whole just twenty years before.[8]

Secondly, there is much greater interconnectedness across the Communion, not least due to the speed of global

8   Archbishop Drexel Gomez, 'On Being Anglican in the 21st Century', address of 26 March 2007 available from: www.globalsouthanglican.org. Jenkins notes that 'the episcopate of what was the "Church of England" now contains a majority of African and Asian clerics. Of 736 bishops registered at Lambeth, only 316 were from the United States, Canada, and Europe combined, while Africa sent 224 and Asia 95' (Jenkins, *The Next Christendom*, p. 236).

communications. While it is has always been true that the action of one member of the body of Christ affects the integrity and health of the whole body (cf. 1 Cor. 12), this is now much more tangible, especially in relation to local mission. One of the most telling exchanges in the Lambeth 1998 debate on sexuality was when Bishop Catherine Roskam of New York responded to the statement of Nigeria's Bishop Peter Adebiyi that any condoning of homosexuality was 'evangelistic suicide'. She stated that 'to condemn it, in the form it has been condemned, is evangelistic suicide in my region'.[9] While clearly such assessments in part simply reflected their different theological outlooks it also in part demonstrates the challenges of contextual mission when our context is one of both globalization of communication and great diversity in cultural context.

Thirdly, the final resolution overwhelmingly passed at that conference at the end of this debate (and it must be recalled

---

9   The West Africa region at the Conference was proposing a resolution (V.35) that sought to amend 1.10 by stating 'This Conference a) noting that – (i) the Word of God has established the fact that God created man and woman and blessed their marriage; (ii) many parts of the Bible condemn homosexuality as a sin; (iii) homosexuality is one of the many sins that Scripture has condemned; (iv) some African Christians in Uganda were martyred in the 19th century for refusing to have homosexual relations with the king because of their faith in the Lord Jesus and their commitment to stand by the Word of God as expressed in the Bible on the subject; (b) stands on the Biblical authority and accepts that homosexuality is a sin which could only be adopted by the church if it wanted to commit evangelical suicide'. This amendment was rejected, though section (f) of the final resolution 'notes the concerns expressed in resolutions IV.26, V.1, V.10, V.23 and V.35 on the authority of Scripture in matters of marriage and sexuality and asks the Primates and the ACC to include them in their monitoring process'.

that even the majority of 'northern' bishops supported the final resolution[10]) clearly stated that the bishops rejected 'homosexual practice as incompatible with Scripture'. While obviously a claim not all would accept,[11] such a judgement does not mark a major break with Christian tradition. Nor is it an unreasonable reading of the biblical texts. In fact it significantly and clearly claims the authority of Scripture for its ethical stance. On these grounds it is in full continuity with Anglican teaching.[12] The Conference was also clear that it 'cannot advise the legitimising or blessing of same sex unions nor ordaining those involved in same gender unions'. Those practical implications were not introduced from the floor but agreed in the motion coming from the subsection on human sexuality.[13]

If the bishops of the Communion gathered in council overwhelmingly agree, in continuity with the wider catholic Church, that certain conduct is 'incompatible with Scripture'

---

10 The figures in the vote for the final resolution were 526–70 with 45 abstentions. Given the figures above (n. 8), it is clear that the total of those unable to support the final motion was equivalent to only about one-third of the 'Northern' bishops present.

11 The amendment was suggested by Archbishop Carey after a number of African leaders expressed concern that unless something like this was carried they would have to support the even stronger statements such as those in V.35 cited above. It was carried by just over two-thirds of those voting – 389–190. See his account in George Carey, *Know the Truth* (London: HarperCollins, 2004), pp. 327ff.

12 It is also in line with earlier Lambeth resolutions on the subject such as 1978 Resolution 10 which reaffirms 'heterosexuality as the scriptural norm'.

13 Apparently the Bishop of Oxford, Richard Harries, 'managed to persuade the sub-section to drop the call for a moratorium on these practices and to use the word advise rather than anything stronger' (John S. Peart-Binns, *A Heart in My Head: A Biography of Richard Harries* (London: Continuum, 2007), p. 199).

and that certain church actions 'cannot be advised' then at the very least a strong signal is being sent as to where the current boundaries of diversity are to be found if we are serious about maintaining unity under the authority of Scripture. That, of course, is what Rowan Williams has consistently said and taken as his principle of action ever since the very day of his appointment. Even though he himself was not a supporter of the original resolution, on his appointment he wrote to his fellow Primates:

> The Lambeth resolution of 1998 declares clearly what is the mind of the overwhelming majority in the Communion, and what the Communion will and will not approve or authorise. I accept that any individual diocese or even province that officially overturns or repudiates this resolution poses a substantial problem for the sacramental unity of the Communion.[14]

Fourthly, events since 1998 have been in sharp contrast to perhaps the most obvious parallel situation in the Communion – that of extending Anglican diversity and testing Anglican unity through ordaining women priests and bishops.[15] There, after the initial ordination of Florence Lei Tim-Oi in 1944, both the Archbishop of Canterbury[16] and the Lambeth

---

14 Archbishop Rowan Williams, Letter to Primates, 23 July 2002.

15 In considering the authority and force of past Lambeth resolutions one might also refer to the even more rigorist 1888 Lambeth resolution that 'persons living in polygamy be not admitted to baptism, but that they be accepted as candidates and kept under Christian instruction until such time as they shall be in a position to accept the law of Christ' (Resolution 5). This was not modified until 1988.

16 William Temple condemned the ordination as 'contrary to the laws and precedents of the church'.

Conference[17] expressed disapproval of this development and she returned her licence. Only after the 1968 Lambeth Conference judged the theological arguments 'inconclusive' (resolution 34) and the 1971 Anglican Consultative Council declared as 'acceptable to this Council' a request to ordain women to the priesthood did any province proceed with such ordinations.[18] Similarly, no women bishops were consecrated until after the 1988 Lambeth Conference recognized this as within the limits of Anglican diversity.[19]

In contrast, since Lambeth 1998, in North America, numerous dioceses, and a whole province, have disregarded the stated mind of the Communion by instituting greater

---

17 Lambeth 1948 Resolution 113 responded to a request from the Chinese church that they have a twenty year experiment by stating 'an experiment would be against the tradition and order and would gravely affect the internal and external relations of the Anglican Communion'. It also (resolution 114) reaffirmed Resolution 67 of the Conference of 1930 that 'the order of deaconess is for women the one and only order of the ministry which we can recommend our branch of the Catholic Church to recognise and use' and approved the resolution adopted in 1939–41 in both Houses of the Convocations of Canterbury and York 'that the order of deaconesses is the one existing ordained ministry for women in the sense of being the only order of ministry in the Anglican Communion to which women are admitted by episcopal imposition of hands'. The Conference also (resolution 115) stated that though 'aware that in some quarters there is a desire that the question of ordination of women to the priesthood should be reconsidered', in the light of the 1935 Church of England Commission report, it was 'of the opinion that the time has not come for its further formal consideration'.

18 The vote, on resolution 28, was very close (24–22 with several abstentions), with the Archbishop of Canterbury voting against.

19 Resolution 1 overwhelmingly (423–28 with 19 abstentions) accepted 'that each province respect the decision and attitudes of other provinces in the ordination or consecration of women to the episcopate'.

diversity through officially sanctioning same-sex blessings and electing, confirming and consecrating as bishop someone in a same gender union.

The underlying central question raised by this chain of events is therefore how we should respond as a Communion when the diversity of accepted practices is extended by the unilateral actions of an autonomous province in disregard for the statements and appeals of the Communion as a whole, especially when the Communion has explicitly reached its judgement on the basis of Scripture. In addition to the 1998 resolution 1.10 on the specific subject of sexuality, the call not to proceed in this way is explicit or implicit in statements by the Archbishop of Canterbury (letters to Primates on 23 July 2002 and 23 July 2003, pre-General Convention), previous Lambeth resolutions,[20] and the decisions of the Anglican Consultative Council.[21]

---

20 For example, 1978 resolution 11 states 'The Conference advises member Churches not to take action regarding issues which are of concern to the whole Anglican Communion without consultation with a Lambeth Conference or with the episcopate through the Primates Committee, and requests the Primates to initiate a study of the nature of authority within the Anglican Communion.' The Episcopal Church itself recognized this principle when in 1991 its General Convention resolved that human sexuality issues were 'potentially divisive issues which should not be resolved by the Episcopal Church on its own' (B020).

21 At the twelfth Meeting in Hong Kong in 2002 resolution 34 was passed stating, 'This Anglican Consultative Council, being concerned about a range of matters of faith and order which have arisen since we last met, and having in mind the constant emphasis on mutual responsibility and interdependence in the resolutions of successive Lambeth Conferences, from the call in 1867 for "unity in faith and discipline by due and canonical subordination of synods" (1867, IV) to the call in 1998 for a "common mind concerning ethical issues where contention threatens to divide" (1998, IV 5 (c)) calls upon: 1. dioceses and individual bishops not to undertake

By focusing in this way (as *The Windsor Report* does) on the *means* by which provinces have acted rather than simply the *actions* they have taken, on the *process* and not primarily the *substance*, it becomes clear that the crisis and many of the major questions it raises about unity and diversity could have been caused by actions in relation to quite different issues. In testing any proposed responses it is therefore helpful not to focus on how they apply to homosexuality, but to ask whether they are transferable and acceptable to other possible extensions of diversity if pursued in a similar manner (that is, contrary to traditional Anglican practice and the stated mind of the Communion through its instruments). One obvious possible example here would be calls in some places for authorization of lay presidency at the Eucharist.

2. Unity and Diversity – Two Flawed Responses

Given this account of where we are and the questions we face, it is important to explore two responses to our current crisis which are often around in the current debate, even if rarely articulated. Both are, I believe, unhelpful and flawed.

One response emphasizes that because Anglicanism has always been diverse and/or that it is inherently inclusive, it therefore follows that what has happened in North America cannot be judged wrong or un-Anglican. It therefore should

---

unilateral actions or adopt policies which would strain our communion with one another without reference to their provincial authorities; and 2. provincial authorities to have in mind the impact of their decisions within the wider Communion; and 3. all members of the Communion, even in our disagreements to have in mind the "need for courtesy, tolerance, mutual respect and prayer for one another" (1998, III.2 (e)).'

not significantly alter relationships and structures within the Communion. Those like me who argue otherwise are, from this perspective, easily seen as intolerant and can often be made to feel that what we are being called to do at this time is simply to learn to live more deeply into our Anglican heritage so as to embrace (or at least tolerate) this new form of diversity that has arisen. If, instead, we oppose these developments and say they have implications for our common life together then this can seem, from this perspective, to be effectively a schismatic attack on Anglican unity.

My problem with this position is in part that it does not seem to make Scripture the authority against which our diversity must be weighed and tested. But it is also that it misses the key point at issue and lacks coherence as a response. It would appear to have to choose between two concrete outworkings of its emphasis on diversity. *Either* this view refuses to set any limits at all to Anglican (or indeed Christian) identity, seeing diversity as infinitely elastic with no impact on Anglicanism's coherence or its unity. This is, in reality, a view that few if any really accept. *Or* its vision and principle of diversity is one which is selectively applied. It is used to justify 'acceptable' diversity (e.g. clergy in same-sex unions but not laity presiding at the Eucharist, or *vice versa*) but the fundamental question of how we discern as a Communion what is legitimate and what is illegitimate development is then left unanswered.

The other position I believe to be flawed holds that the limits of Anglican diversity have been so clearly defined and established in such sufficient detail once and for all (perhaps in Scripture, perhaps in tradition) that any debate about them or proposed developments relating to them, whether in doctrine or practice, matters of faith or matters of order, can be judged illegitimate *a priori*. From this perspective, when such debate or development occurs it amounts to an abandonment of truth and a schismatic attack on the Church's unity – for the true schismatic is the one who causes separation, not necessarily the one who separates. In this understanding we supposedly already know – apart from common counsel and discernment – clearly and definitively whether any issue is 'first order' or 'second order', whether it is 'core and essential' or 'indifferent' and 'adiaphora'. This view can, in its most rigorist form, even make it a 'first order' and hence 'communion-breaking' issue if someone simply questions whether a claimed first order issue really is that important.

My concern here is that theologically this appears to have an over-realized eschatology. It forgets that the Church is not yet free from sin and that we still only see in a mirror dimly and know only in part. It also denies the Reformation principle that the Church, having been reformed, should always go on being reformed (*ecclesia reformata semper reformanda*).[22] Paradoxically, given the claims of some of its adherents, it also risks replacing the Word of God with human constructs.

Practically, of course, this view is also often a threat to the Church's unity. Disagreements over the limits of diversity lead to division but those who disagree with a development and separate off soon find themselves further dividing over other matters. The dangerous consequences of this outlook are perhaps best captured in what the Ship of Fools website voted as the funniest religious joke:

A man was walking across a bridge one day, and saw a man standing on the edge, about to jump. He ran over and said: 'Stop. Don't do it.'

---

22   For discussion of this using Calvin's critique of traditional teaching on usury see my 'Semper Reformanda in a Changing World: Calvin, Usury and Evangelical Moral Theology', in Sung Wook Chung (ed.), *Alister E McGrath and Evangelical Theology: A Dynamic Engagement* (Carlisle: Paternoster Press, 2003), pp. 235–63 and available at www.fulcrum-anglican.org.uk

'Why shouldn't I?' he asked.

'Well, there's so much to live for!'

'Like what?'

'Are you religious?'

'Yes.'

'Me too. Are you Christian or Buddhist?'

'Christian.'

'Me too. Are you Catholic or Protestant?'

'Protestant.'

'Me too. Are you Anglican or Baptist?'

'Baptist.'

'Wow. Me too. Are you Baptist Church of God or Baptist Church of the Lord?'

'Baptist Church of God.'

'Me too. Are you original Baptist Church of God, or are you Reformed Baptist Church of God?'

'Reformed Baptist Church of God.'

'Me too. Are you Reformed Baptist Church of God, Reformation of 1879, or Reformed Baptist Church of God, Reformation of 1915?'

He said: 'Reformed Baptist Church of God, Reformation of 1915.'

At which point the conversation ended with the cry 'Die, heretic scum,' as the passer-by pushed the man off the bridge.[23]

Historically, of course, this outlook fails to do justice to the Church's shifting understanding, especially on moral issues. It is clear that in relation to (for example) divorce and remarriage, contraception and the proper pattern of discipline

---

23 Text (and links to others in the top 10 funniest and top 10 offensive religious jokes) at: www.ship-of-fools.com/Features/2005/ laugh_judgment_results.html

in response to polygamy, Anglicanism has developed. While some will believe at least some of these developments are false steps, the point is that unless as a Communion we believe that all change is wrong – the polar opposite of the first viewpoint that to welcome all changes seems unquestioningly within autonomous provinces – we need some means to discern together in common council which changes are good and Spirit-led reformations, and which are worldly (in the negative Johannine sense) damaging deformations of God's people and departures from Scripture.

The problem with both these perspectives is therefore similar – they are mirror-images of each other – and neither offers a constructive way forward together. They respond to the historical and imperfect nature of the church either by appealing to some general abstract principle of inclusion or diversity or by insisting on some clearly defined template. There is a tendency to strong confidence in a particular view of God's providence in history. The first approach tends to see human history as progress (perhaps appealing to Christ's words that 'the Spirit leads us into all truth') whereas the other tends to see history in terms of departure and decline from some golden era.

Instead of either of these approaches it is necessary to develop a way in which we order our life together so we can be guided – by Word and Spirit – to walk together. Paul's closing words to the Thessalonians are perhaps particularly apt here:

> Live in peace with each other. … be patient with everyone. Make sure that nobody pays back wrong for wrong, but always try to be kind to each other and to everyone else. Be joyful always; pray continually; give thanks in all circumstances, for this is God's will for you in Christ Jesus. Do not put out the Spirit's fire; do not treat prophecies with contempt. Test everything.

Hold on to the good. Avoid every kind of evil. May God himself, the God of peace, sanctify you through and through. May your whole spirit, soul and body be kept blameless at the coming of our Lord Jesus Christ. The one who calls you is faithful and he will do it.[24]

3. Communion & Covenant – The Way Forward Together?

What might that mean for us in the Anglican Communion at this present time? I want to suggest that we may best find a way forward together through exploring the twin themes of communion and covenant. These are, of course, at the forefront of much political and institutional discussion at present but I want to argue that we cannot just approach the challenges we face and consider these two terms simply at the pressing practical level. Before looking at the specific concrete issue of an Anglican Covenant I want to sketch a theological and ecclesiological framework before, finally, recalling that what must undergird and guide all of this is the mission of God and of the Church.

Theology – Communion and Covenant

Before speaking of the Anglican Communion, or communion within the church more broadly, we need to begin with the triune God and his mission to redeem his creation and restore us to communion with himself. Before *looking around* and thinking of relationships of communion among ourselves we need to *look up* and consider the relationship of communion with God and so also *look out* to the world where we are called

---

24   1 Thess. 5.13–24 (NIV).

61

to share in God's mission. We need to emphasize that our communion with one another is a gift which is established in and through Christ. And at its heart is our sharing together in God's gracious communion with us in Christ. Such communion theology and ecclesiology is now well established in Anglicanism and wider ecumenical (particularly Roman Catholic) ecclesiology. It is at the heart of *The Windsor Report* and space prevents further exploration of it here.

The language and theology of covenant is much less prominent in Anglican theology or ecclesiology although it plays an important role in other traditions.[25] As someone brought up in the Church of Scotland, the Reformed tradition of covenant theology and the covenant of grace have always been important to me and, as Paul Fiddes' recent illuminating work has demonstrated, covenant is particularly notable in Baptist ecclesiology.[26] Who knows, perhaps as Anglicans we can, through our current difficulties, help to develop a contemporary ecclesiology which is truly both Catholic and Reformed, both communion-centred and covenantal?

Developing a theology of covenant is not only important because we are now rapidly proceeding with the creation of an Anglican Covenant.[27] It is important because biblically and

---

25 Important recent studies from a more evangelical perspective include Mark J. Cartledge and David Mills (eds), *Covenant Theology: Contemporary Approaches* (Carlisle: Paternoster, 2001); Jamie A. Grant and Alistair I. Wilson, *The God of Covenant: Biblical, Theological and Contemporary Perspectives* (Leicester: Apollos, 2005) and Petrus J. Gräbe, *New Covenant, New Community: The Significance of Biblical and Patristic Covenant Theology for Contemporary Understanding* (Carlisle: Paternoster, 2006).

26 Paul Fiddes, *Tracks and Traces: Baptist Identity in Church and Theology* (Studies in Baptist History and Thought Volume 13) (Carlisle: Paternoster, 2003).

27 The conference at which this chapter was originally presented took place immediately following the meeting of the Covenant Design

theologically covenant is such a central theme and so intimately linked to communion. Indeed, if we are to avoid some of the errors that can creep into communion ecclesiology when too close a parallel is drawn between divine communion among the persons of the Trinity and God's communion with us or our human communion within Christ's body, then a theology of covenant could prove most helpful.

The informative Anchor Bible Dictionary article on covenant begins with the following explanation:

> A 'covenant' is an agreement enacted between two parties in which one or both make promises under oath to perform or refrain from certain actions stipulated in advance. As indicated by the designation of the two sections of the Christian Bible – Old Testament (= covenant) and New Testament – 'covenant' in the Bible is the major metaphor used to describe the relation between God and Israel (the people of God). As such, covenant is the instrument constituting the rule (or kingdom) of God, and therefore it is a valuable lens through which one can recognize and appreciate the biblical ideal of religious community.[28]

In the Old Testament the key Hebrew word for covenant – *berith* – appears 287 times and most importantly in the so-called 'covenant formula' – 'I will take you as my people, and I will be your God' or 'I will be your God, and you shall be my

---

Group who, at their meeting, produced a draft covenant which was subsequently commended by the Primates' Meeting in February 2007.

28 George A. Mendenhall and Gary A. Herion, 'Covenant', in *Anchor Bible Dictionary* (New York: Doubleday, 1992, CD edition).

people'. This appears first at Exod. 6.7 and reappears in similar form not only in the Pentateuch (e.g. Lev. 26.12, Deut. 26.17–19, 29.12–13) but the historical books (such as 2 Sam. 7.24) and the prophets (in Jeremiah, Ezekiel and Zechariah).[29] Here we see that the covenant is both the *means* and also the *expression* of God's will for communion. Indeed the Old Testament is the history of God's mission of covenant-making – with Noah, Abraham, Moses, David, etc. – and Israel's regular history of covenant-breaking. That story reaches its climax of course in the fulfilment of the promised 'new covenant' in Christ – 'this is my blood of the new covenant' – and by the Spirit.

Given that our current disputes are focused on sexuality it might also perhaps prove of interest that the language of covenant is tied to that of marriage both in Scripture and Christian tradition – especially the Reformed tradition.[30] And of course some seeking recognition for a form of holy same-sex union have often looked to this category as a fruitful biblical and theological one, as seen in the covenant between David and Jonathan. G. R. Dunstan, in an old sermon exploring marriage as covenant, highlights several features of God's covenants in Scripture that may perhaps also help us when we turn to think of ecclesiological rather than divine or marital

---

29 See discussion of David L. Baker, 'Covenant: an Old Testament Study' in Grant and Wilson, *The God of Covenant*, pp. 21–53.

30 See, for example, John Witte Jr., *From Sacrament to Contract: Marriage, Religion, and Law in the Western Tradition* (Louisville: Westminster John Knox, 1997), especially ch. 3 ('Marriage as covenant in the Calvinist tradition') and John Witte Jr and Eliza Ellison (eds), *Covenant Marriage in Comparative Perspective* (Grand Rapids: Eerdmans, 2005).

covenants.[31] First, the covenant is an initiative of love inviting
a response. Second, it is secured by an oath or vow. Third, it
entails obligations of faithfulness. Fourth, it contains promises
of blessing and fifth it is marked by sacrifice. Those, then, are
some of the hallmarks of God's covenantal activity towards us
as he establishes communion with us in history. They may in
turn shape our own covenant-making, communion-building
activity towards one another.

Within covenant theology, one of the key debates is the
extent to which God's covenants are unconditional and in
what sense they are conditional on particular obedient human
responses. Once again this cannot be explored in detail here
but, given the depth of the current crisis in Anglicanism, it is
important to note that even in the New Testament there is a
frightening recognition that those in a covenanted communion
relationship with God can, through persistent disobedience
and hard-heartedness, fall under divine judgement.

Paul famously warns the church in Corinth that they need to
learn from Israel's history of covenant-breaking:

> Our forefathers were all under the cloud and they all
> passed through the sea. They were all baptised into
> Moses in the cloud and in the sea. They all ate the
> same spiritual food and drank the same spiritual drink.
> … Nevertheless, God was not pleased with most of
> them; their bodies were scattered over the desert.[32]

That warns us that if we are to be faithful to Scripture we also
need to have an ecclesiology able to recognize that we can, as

---

31 G. R. Dunstan, 'The Marriage Covenant: Sermon Preached Before
the University of Cambridge, Sunday, 13 November 1960', in
Theology 78 (May 1975), pp. 244–52.

32 1 Cor. 10.1–5 (NIV).

local churches as well as individuals, disobey and diverge from God's path of communion. Paul's warning seems also to say that, though vitally important and necessary, it is not sufficient (and may be unwise and dangerous) to reduce our understanding of communion solely to the established and received gift of a covenantal status and communion relationship in Christ which is secured and nourished through our common baptism and shared Eucharist.

And that warning is always addressed first and foremost to us and not to others in the Church. It is a danger deep in ourselves – as Paul writes in 1 Cor. 10.12 – 'if you think you are standing firm, be careful that you do not fall!' Or as he warns the Gentiles in Romans 11:

> Do not be arrogant, but be afraid. For if God did not spare the natural branches, he will not spare you either. Consider therefore the kindness and sternness of God: sternness to those who fell, but kindness to you, provided that you continue in his kindness. Otherwise, you also will be cut off.[33]

Lack of kindness, arrogance about one's own security and rejecting and looking down on the part of God's people are – in other words – ultimately attitudes and patterns of behaviour incompatible with life in communion within God's covenant and will lead to divine judgement.

Ecclesiology – Covenanted Life Together in Communion

That rather frightening passage from Romans highlights that there is an intimate connection between God's covenantal action towards us and how we are to act towards one another. We need, then, to comment briefly on some principles of life

---

33   Rom. 11.22–3 (NIV).

together and how a communion-centred and covenant-centred approach may guide these and so shape the more specific relational and concrete political challenges of the Anglican Communion.

I want briefly to note two characteristics of life in communion I think particularly relevant at this time and then again say a little more about how deepening our understanding of covenant may help.

First, communion theology and ecclesiology remind us that we do not set the agenda and that communion is not our project which we are free to create and develop as we wish. We are bound to one another by God himself, knitted together in Christ as members of his body, and indwelt by his Spirit so as to become the temple of God. In the words of *The Windsor Report*:

> As we Anglicans face very serious challenges to our unity and communion in Christ – challenges which have emerged not least because of different interpretations of that holiness to which we are called, and different interpretations of the range of appropriate diversity within our union and communion – Paul would want to remind us of the unique source of that unity, our common identity in Christ, and its unique purpose, the furtherance of God's mission within the world. We too have certainly been gifted with the grace of fellowship with God the Father, God the Son, and God the Holy Spirit. We are, by God's gift, in communion with the Persons of the Holy Trinity, and are members of one another in Christ Jesus. We are, in the power of the Spirit, sent into all the world to declare that Jesus is Lord. This grace-given and grace-full mission from God, and communion with God, determine our relationship

with one another. Communion with God and one another in Christ is thus both a gift and a divine expectation. All that we say in this report is intended both to celebrate that gift and to answer that expectation.[34]

This understanding is particularly important to emphasize if we speak of covenant. There is the danger that covenant language becomes contractual language and (especially when it is stressed this is an 'opt-in' covenant[35]) it can easily become a matter of human will. It could further degenerate into a case of simply joining together with like-minded people to achieve particular ends, perhaps in intentional hostility towards others who own the name of Christ. However, theologically we have seen that God's work of communion is accomplished by means of covenant and any ecclesial covenant we create in order to express and encourage communion among ourselves must therefore be founded in and shaped by the character of God's initiating work of establishing communion with us and among us.

One consequence of this is the recognition that whatever we mean when we talk politically of 'provincial autonomy' it

---

34 *TWR* §5.

35 'The idea of a "covenant" between local Churches (developing alongside the existing work being done on harmonizing the church law of different local Churches) is one method that has been suggested, and it seems to me the best way forward. It is necessarily an "opt-in" matter. Those Churches that were prepared to take this on as an expression of their responsibility to each other would limit their local freedoms for the sake of a wider witness; and some might not be willing to do this' (Archbishop Rowan Williams, 'Challenge and Hope').

cannot be independence or sovereignty.[36] Any 'autonomy' in the church must always be set within, and be defined and limited by, the sort of vision of inter-dependent communion that Paul gives when he later warns the Corinthians – 'The eye cannot say to the hand, "I don't need you!" And the head cannot say to the feet, "I don't need you!"' (1 Cor. 12.21). That is not, of course, to say that anything goes, that all that happens in the body of Christ, every form of diversity, is acceptable. Earlier in the letter he has gone so far as to discipline through ex-communication someone living in gross immorality (1 Cor. 5) and he proceeds to give instructions on how there has to be orderly worship (1 Cor. 14). He also has demonstrated another practical implication of such interdependence and mutual love and accountability in relation to the Lord's Supper – 'when you come together to eat, wait for each other' (1 Cor. 11.33) – in a passage appealed to by the Archbishop of Canterbury in his letter to Primates before the 2003 General Convention.[37]

Here we find the second aspect of life in communion that needs to be emphasized, the necessary Christian virtue, the form of love of neighbour, that is required if we are to fulfil God's calling to live in communion, to live together in

---

36 This is a central argument of *TWR*, especially §§72–86. It was more fully explored and defended in Norman Doe's important work for the Lambeth Commission, 'Communion and Autonomy in Anglicanism: Nature and Maintenance' available at:
http://www.aco.org/commission/documents/autonomy.pdf

37 'We do not have a central executive authority in our Communion; this means we are quite vulnerable in times of deep disagreement, and need more than ever to pay attention to one another. St Paul says in I Corinthians 11:33: "When you gather together to eat the Lord's Supper, wait for one another." We all need to ponder how this may apply to our situations' (Letter to Primates, 23 July 2003).

interdependence and mutual respect and submission. It is the virtue of patience.

Although I and many others think that the actions of the American Church were primarily wrong in substance, the reason there is even wider and deeper unhappiness in the Communion as a whole is that they were also wrong in terms of process, given the Christian disciplines of interdependent life in communion. That is the primary criticism offered by *The Windsor Report* and the Instruments of Communion. The danger now, particularly after the request made by the Primates in Tanzania, is that if we are unable even to accept that there has been a significant false step (and a breach in the bonds of affection in that sense) then there is little hope of staying together and framing a covenant that can help us find a way forward together. There is little hope because we ultimately then discover that we have incompatible understandings of the nature of the Christian life, which we have been called to live together as a communion of churches.

But if the pattern of divine action in covenant and communion, rather than any agendas of our own, must shape our activity within the Church as we covenant with one another then the quality of patience must also be exercised by the wider Communion in response to The Episcopal Church. The pattern of God's covenant love is one of patient forbearance. In Romans 2 Paul talks of God's 'kindness, tolerance and patience' in order to lead us to repentance. Despite the difficulties, and interventions within the United States by some bishops, in many ways such patience and forbearance has been shown for a considerable time. Similarly, in asking for clarifications from the American Church, the Primates in Tanzania were acknowledging that, given God graciously perseveres in seeking his goal of communion with us, we also need to learn patience with each other.

That principle also means that if there is no regret for breaching the bonds of affection and no commitment to a moratorium on unilateral actions against the mind of the Communion then whatever form Communion discipline takes, it must – like all church discipline – seek to be a means of grace in order to restore communion through amendment of life and not a means of humiliation or irrevocable separation. This principle is written into the draft covenant where, rather than establishing elaborate punitive processes and judicial procedures for those breaking the covenant, it is proposed that those making covenant with each other include within their commitment a recognition that:

> In the most extreme circumstances, where member churches choose not to fulfil the substance of the covenant as understood by the Councils of the Instruments of Communion, we will consider that such churches will have relinquished for themselves the force and meaning of the covenant's purpose, and a process of restoration and renewal will be required to re-establish their covenant relationship with other member churches.[38]

In what other ways – if Windsor is right that the 'grace-given and grace-full mission from God, and communion with God, determine our relationship with one another' – might a biblical theology of covenant help shape a response? One problem is that Scripture's focus is on God's covenant with us whereas we

---

38 Anglican Communion Office, *An Anglican Covenant: A Draft for Discussion* (April 2007), §6.6, available at: http://www.anglicancommunion.org/commission/d_covenant/docs/Draft%20Covenant%20Text%20070504.pdf

are looking now at a covenant among ourselves. But that does not make Scriptural references to covenant of no value.

Firstly, there are also in Scripture numerous covenants between people – both individuals and groups. Again they are scattered throughout the OT – Abraham and Abimelech in Genesis 21, Jacob and Laban in Genesis 31, David and Abner in 2 Samuel 3. Secondly, the use of covenant language within Israel is clearly a divine appropriation of the widespread social phenomenon. This was such that the *Anchor Bible Dictionary* says of covenants: 'As instruments for the creation and regulation of relationships between different social groups, they seem to have been universal in the ancient world.'[39] Although God's covenant with his people was unique and distinctive, the concept only made sense because of that wider context of covenants in which the parties committed themselves to a certain relationship and certain obligations to each other. Thirdly, and most importantly, if covenant is the means of God expressing and establishing and enabling his will for communion with us, it is a particularly appropriate form for us to express, establish and enable our will for communion with one another.

Establishing a covenant is of course a significant development. For some, it challenges how we have expressed our life together in the past. It must, however, be recognized that the current crisis reveals that the old ways are no longer working as well as they did and many have valid questions about them. We must remember that the worldwide Anglican Communion grew out of a national established church's missionary endeavours from within the culture of Christendom and in the context of imperialism. That ecclesiological and wider political context is no longer our reality. We might also

---

39 Mendenhall and Herion, 'Covenant', in *Anchor Bible Dictionary*, CD edition.

reasonably suspect that such a context significantly constrained or even distorted our theological imagination and understanding of what it means to be the Church.

Traditionally, one of Anglicanism's distinctive and valuable features has been its decentralized understanding of authority and its emphasis on establishing national churches which understood, expressed and lived the gospel in mission to their own cultures. But, as so often, there are also dangers and weaknesses arising out of and reflecting these strengths. First, perhaps each church's polity and political culture simply uncritically follows that of their society and does not understand other Anglican polities and cultures.[40] Second, the Communion has lacked a clearly articulated understanding of its own life together. This common life has worked on the basis of a mixture of the good English habit of an unwritten constitution based on gentlemen's agreements and conventions and a United Nations-style statement of collective goals and commitments combined with a policy of non-interference within the internal affairs of each autonomous province. The development of the Instruments – most recently the Anglican Consultative Council and then the Primates' Meeting – has created more room for common council but the role and significance of that remains unacknowledged in the internal life of each of the provinces and (especially given the speed of global communication) in a time of crisis the Instruments struggle to keep pace with events and reactions to them.

In such a situation, to enter into a covenant with each other has much to commend it. It should not replace the bonds of affection for chains of law (as it has sometimes been put) but

---

40 Alleged ignorance of their distinctive polity has been a major complaint made by the American Church in response to the Anglican Primates' requests, although the rhetoric here is greater than the substance.

rather – as in Scripture – express and articulate what those bonds of affection mean and how they shape our relationships with each other: covenant as expression of communion and ordered towards deeper communion.

Recalling the features of God's covenant outlined by Dunstan, this must be an initiative of love inviting a response and promising blessing. Part of the problem at present is that it is not being seen as such in some quarters. Indeed at times it is almost being seen as a means of enforcing and institution-alizing divisions.[41] Any covenant also requires explicit and solemn commitments and these must be shaped by a Scriptural vision of life in communion.[42] A covenant also entails serious obligations of faithfulness to one another. Undoubtedly one of the problems at present is that people have felt misled – even betrayed and deceived – by some of their fellow Anglicans and any covenant must work to overcome these problems, prevent their repetition, and so rebuild mutual trust. But, finally, neither can it be forgotten that biblical covenant is marked by sacrifice and covenant-making will be costly to all parties (some perhaps more obviously than others at this initial stage). This is a cost that some may be unwilling to pay either now or in the future.[43]

41 The presentation on the covenant by Katherine Grieb (a member of the Covenant Design Group) to the American House of Bishops presented such a negative assessment as – despite her initial support for the draft covenant – she argued that it now needed to be interpreted through her (mis-)reading of the Primates' Communiqué from Tanzania.

42 The draft covenant appears (though its current structure masks this in places) to offer a pattern of affirmations and commitments in relation to confession of faith (§§2, 3), mission (§4) and unity (§§5, 6).

43 Here there needs to be more work done in relation to the idea that the covenant will result – to some degree – in a distinction between 'constituent' and 'associate' Anglicans.

Politics – Instruments of Communion and The Anglican Covenant

So what might this mean concretely for the Anglican Communion? Clearly the logic of this argument is that the Covenant Design Group has important work to do which must not simply focus on addressing the current crisis but be determined by theological and ecclesiological understandings of communion and covenant. It must however also face the reality of our current situation and address the issue of unity and diversity. In part 2, I sketched two unhelpful approaches, both of which have been vocal in discussion of the covenant. The first – with its belief in diversity as a defining hallmark of Anglicanism – leads either to a rejection of any covenant or to as minimalist a covenant as possible, one focused more on aspirations and ethos and less on agreed processes and substance.[44] The second – with its clarity over the fixed limits of diversity – leads to a strongly confessional covenant being proposed. While any covenant must include aspirational, ethical and confessional elements it must not be reduced to them. At its heart must instead lie a way of addressing how as a communion of churches we recognize all that we have in common and how we can maintain our unity as we discern together the limits of diversity and respond to those who fracture our unity by breaching those agreed limits.

Given our recent history, the answer lies neither in autonomy understood as independence, nor in instituting – as some fear – some new hierarchical, papal or curial

---

44 One example of this sort of response to the covenant proposal is that offered by the Modern Churchpeople's Union and available from: www.modchurchunion.org/Publications/Papers/Covenant/Summ ary%20response.htm. It is in line with their earlier book: Jonathan Clatworthy and David Taylor (eds), *The Windsor Report – A Liberal Response* (Winchester: O Books, 2005).

international jurisdiction. It must instead focus on the importance of our common council together rooted in shared worship and reading of Scripture, our mutual listening to one another as we seek the mind of Christ and our respect within provinces for the mind of the Communion on the limits of diversity when these are clearly expressed. The fulfilment of these tasks has increasingly been recognised as crucial in the Communion and the proposed draft covenant suggests this is the path that will be followed.

Recently it is to the Primates' Meetings that many have looked for answers to our current crisis and the draft covenant in its most controversial section gives it a specific and significant role. It is, though, important to be clear that what the draft covenant proposes is in line with recent developments and decisions by the Instruments and is not as radical a shift as some have understood.

At the Lambeth Conference of 1988 a resolution was passed (18.2) which urged 'that encouragement be given to a developing collegial role for the Primates' Meeting under the presidency of the Archbishop of Canterbury, so that the Primates' Meeting is able to exercise an enhanced responsibility in offering guidance on doctrinal, moral and pastoral matters'. In 1998 this was reaffirmed with the added request that the Primates undertake the 'giving of guidelines on the limits of Anglican diversity in submission to the sovereign authority of Holy Scripture and in loyalty to our Anglican tradition and formularies' (III.6). In practice, in various ways,[45] culminating with the decisions at Tanzania, the Primates have fulfilled these requests of the Conference.

---

45 Following the 2000 Porto statement ('we believe that the unity of the Communion as a whole still rests on the Lambeth Quadrilateral. ... Only a formal and public repudiation of this would place a diocese or Province outside the Anglican Communion') and the 2002 Canterbury Statement on the doctrine of God, this role has been

In the light of this it is, therefore, reasonable for the covenant to respond to the need of providing a way for the Communion truly to submit together to Scripture and remain loyal to Anglican tradition and formularies. The draft covenant does not propose the Communion give power or authority to define and enforce the limits of Anglican diversity to the Primates. It does though propose that churches covenant with one another to 'seek the guidance of the Instruments of Communion, where there are matters in serious dispute among churches that cannot be resolved by mutual admonition and counsel' and to do so 'by submitting the matter to the Primates' Meeting'. But 'if the Primates believe that the matter is not one for which a common mind has been articulated, they will seek it with the other instruments and their councils' and not on their own. Even when such a common mind is discerned, the Primates will continue simply to 'offer guidance and direction'.

Covenant has, as noted earlier, been important in Baptist thinking. Paul Fiddes identifies Gainsborough in 1606 or 1607 as particularly formative for Baptist Christians. There a congregation of English Separatists covenanted together in a manner subsequently described in the following way – they

> joined themselves (by a covenant of the Lord) into a Church estate, in the fellowship of the gospel, to walk in all his ways, made known, or to be made known

---

particularly evident in relation to sexuality and the current crisis. This has been shown from the meeting in Brazil in 2003 to the special Lambeth meeting later that year (which included the statement 'As Primates of our Communion seeking to exercise the 'enhanced responsibility' entrusted to us by successive Lambeth Conferences ...') and Dromantine in 2005 (which established the Panel of Reference), which called on the American and Canadian churches to withdraw their representatives from the forthcoming ACC in Nottingham.

unto them, according to their best endeavours, whatsoever it should cost them, the Lord assisting them.[46]

In the early seventeenth century for a group of local Christians it was comparatively easy to work out how they would discern the ways of the Lord made known or to be made known unto them (although, as Fiddes notes, that did not prevent early divisions appearing among them!). For Anglicans as a global Communion in the twenty-first century the processes and structures by which we do that are much more difficult to determine. Nobody would claim the existing ones are perfect. But they are currently the only ones we have. If we are committed to life in communion and walking together, rather than learning to walk apart, then we are now at a point where we need to covenant with one another to use them, to reform them, but also to respect their considered judgements 'whatsoever it should cost'. Those unable to make such commitments or who do so but then find themselves unable to keep them are not thereby unchurched and cut off from Christ. They do, however, thereby place themselves in a different relationship with those who can make and keep such commitments to each other.

For whatever reasons, some churches may be unwilling to covenant to the degree of fullness of communion and pattern of patient forbearance and mutual interdependence which is being proposed. As a result they can no longer expect to share in common counsel and discernment in the same way. They will become perhaps more like ecumenical partners and observers rather than fellow Anglicans, having chosen to

---

46 Description of William Bradford, cited in Fiddes, *Tracks and Traces*, p. 21.

accept what has been called 'associate' rather than 'constituent' status.

Mission – Covenanted Communion for the Sake of the World

Finally, the danger is that the current crisis and responses to it can become simply a matter of navel-gazing, internal house-keeping. The theological starting-point, however, was that we need to set all discussion of communion and covenant in the context of God and his mission to the world and the acknowledgment that the Church is God's agent of mission in the world. That mission is one of establishing communion and God's means in this mission is his covenant-making. Our concern with ecclesiological and institutional and relational matters is because, as God's covenant people, the Church is called to make known before the world, in word and in deed, the pattern of God's will for communion in Christ that promises to unite together diverse peoples under the Lordship of Christ.

The real danger we now face is that if the limits to our diversity are not subject to our common counsel, if we fail to give due weight to the effect that actions by Anglicans in one place have on mission by Anglicans in another, and if we cannot pause and take stock when some see our differences to be so great as to amount to different gospels, then we will do more than deny the nature of communion. We will risk losing a common vision of God's mission in which we are called to share and in which we need one another if we are to hear and be faithful to God's call.

As we move towards the next Lambeth Conference planned for 2008 and we continue work on a covenant for the Communion, what is needed above all is a missional mindset which must frame and shape and direct all thinking and planning relating to covenant and communion. Here the final words of *The Windsor Report* speak a prophetic challenge to Anglicans across the Communion:

> The real challenge of the gospel is whether we live deeply enough in the love of Christ, and care sufficiently for our joint work to bring that love to the world, that we will 'make every effort to maintain the unity of the Spirit in the bond of peace' (Eph. 4.3). As the primates stated in 2000, 'to turn from one another would be to turn away from the Cross', and indeed from serving the world which God loves and for which Christ died.[47]

---

47   *TWR* §157.

3

The Dull Bits of History: Cautionary Tales for Anglicanism

MARK D. CHAPMAN

Sometimes the study of history can be immensely dull. Writing of the political thought of the middle ages, the great scholar-monk, J. N. Figgis, a man never prone to understatement, claimed that it was a study based on a 'literature without charm or brilliancy or overmuch eloquence, voluminous, arid, scholastic, for the most part; dead it seems beyond any language ever spoken. Dust and ashes seem arguments, illustrations, standpoints, and even personalities.'[1] Nevertheless, he held, the political theories of the Middle Ages and early modern period possessed what he called a 'significant dullness'.[2] This was an approach to history that Figgis shared with his teacher, Mandell Creighton, the great

---

1   J. N. Figgis, *Studies in Political Thought from Gerson to Grotius* (Cambridge: Cambridge University Press, 1907), p. 2. See also Figgis, 'Political Thought in the Sixteenth Century', in *Cambridge Modern History* in Lord Acton (ed.) *Cambridge Modern History* (Cambridge: Cambridge University Press, 1904), vol. iii, pp. 736–769; 'Politics at the Council of Constance,' in *Transactions of the Royal Historical Society* NS13 (1899), pp. 103–15. On Figgis as a historian see Mark Goldie, 'J. N. Figgis and the History of Political Thought in Cambridge', in Richard Mason (ed.), *Cambridge Minds* (Cambridge: Cambridge University Press, 1994), pp. 177–92. See also my *Bishops, Saints and Politics* (London: T & T Clark, 2007), chapter 4.

2   Figgis, *Gerson to Grotius*, p. 2.

historian of the medieval papacy, who wrote in the preface to his multi-volume work on the fifteenth- and sixteenth-century Popes: 'Much that is interesting has been omitted, much that is dull has been told at length. My omissions and my details are intentional. I have enlarged on points, not because they are interesting to the modern observer, but because they formed part of the political experience of those who moulded the immediate future.'[3] Figgis went even further in asserting the world-historical significance of the period of the councils. Writing in 1907, he said:

> Probably the most revolutionary official document in the history of the world is the decree of the Council of Constance asserting its superiority to the Pope, and striving to turn into a tepid constitutionalism the Divine authority of a thousand years. The [conciliar] movement is the culmination of medieval constitutionalism. It forms the watershed between the medieval and the modern world. We see in the struggle of the movement the herald of the struggle between constitutional principles, and the claims of autocracy in the State, which was, save in [England] and the Netherlands, to conclude by the triumph of the latter and the riveting of despotism upon the people until the upheaval of the French revolution.[4]

It is unlikely that any historian writing in the future about *The Windsor Report* will make this kind of assertion for the importance of the contemporary debates in the Anglican Communion. Nevertheless there may be a footnote to some

---

3   Mandell Creighton, *History of the Papacy from the Great Schism to the Sack of Rome* (London: Longmans, 1909), i, pp. v, vii. On Creighton, see my *Bishops, Saints and Politics*, chapter 6.

4   Figgis, *Gerson to Grotius*, p. 35.

learned tome regretting the historical inadequacies of the Report and its failure to engage adequately with the dull bits of the past, not least those periods where councils were convoked with the express intention of removing schism and defeating heresy. Consequently, even if the Council of Constance was not quite the world-historical event that Figgis claimed (and, besides, he was arguing a different point), it comes as something of a surprise that it does not feature at all in *The Windsor Report* – and neither for that matter do any of the other medieval councils.

My claim in this paper is that advocates of the expansion and development of Anglican conciliarism (which seems to be the implication of the recent discussions about the need for some sort of Anglican Covenant) might have something to learn from both the successes and failures of medieval conciliarism. Indeed, it is important to note that the development of the Church of England, and the churches across the world that eventually emerged from that Church, was intimately connected with the conflicts, schisms and debates that accompanied the clamour for power and authority in the late middle ages. What is crucial for those involved in the production of a Covenant is to give some attention to the kind of 'tepid constitutionalism' that emerged in the fifteenth century. While often laudable in its ideals, conciliarism lacked sufficient support in both church and state to achieve its aims. In the end it proved singularly ineffective as other, somewhat more centralized, models of ecclesiastical authority and sovereignty developed. Sometimes pragmatism might be a more sensible solution than idealism.

Conciliarism and the Council of Constance

Although it would not be possible to go into all the details of the conciliar period, which Figgis is accurate in regarding as fairly dull, there are nevertheless a few key points to note about the Council of Constance which I will discuss in this section. Precisely how these are relevant for the discussion of a proposed Covenant for the Anglican Communion will emerge through the course of the paper. The Council was held between 1414 and 1418 and was aimed at ending the Great Schism of the western Church, which had begun in 1378, when the church was divided between two rival popes, Urban VI, the initial Roman claimant, and Clement VII, who was elected after signs of mental instability in Urban, and who set up his court at Avignon. The effort to unite the church at the Council at Pisa in 1409 led to yet another papal claimant, Alexander V. Each claimant established a succession, and papal history in these years is correspondingly complex. Such a situation could hardly be regarded as strengthening the standing of the church in its struggles with the state, which meant something had to be done. Besides, a number of reformers, including Wycliffe in England and Huss in Bohemia had been questioning some of the long-cherished teachings of the Church. Consequently, the Council of Constance was convened to put an end to this division in Christendom, as well as to silence the Hussites and to attempt to reform the Church 'in head and members'.

Where much energy before the fourteenth century had been devoted to the competing claims of church and state or empire, the conflicts moved in the later fourteenth century towards the internal divisions of the church. The doctrine of the Church – what was much later to be called ecclesiology – became fundamental. Historians of the Church tend to date the beginnings of the '*prehistory* of ecclesiology' to as late as the thirteenth century – before that there was remarkably little reflection on the nature and structure of the Church. Indeed, the standard medieval text book of theology, which all aspiring clergy were expected to study, the *Sentences* of Peter Lombard, who died in 1160, does not even contain a separate section on the doctrine of the Church.[5] Provoked by issues of heresy, but also over the relative claims of the national bishops and churches, and the central church governed by the Pope, ecclesiology became a key topic of conversation and theological debate in the following centuries. How the periphery related to the centre was crucial. There was a host of other problems as well, not least the nature of the relationships between the Pope and his cardinals, who were frequently conceived as a kind of council of advice. The old third-century struggles between the relative claims of Cyprian and Pope Stephen,[6] and the ideal of universal jurisdiction from the centre over the whole church, were magnified in the transformed European situation and the universal claims of Christianity in what had become known as Christendom.

Although papal claims to jurisdictional authority had gradually developed from the time of Gregory VII in the eleventh century through to the Fourth Lateran Council of 1215, there was continued controversy over the rights of the papacy in relation to other centres of power through the later middle ages. Conflict frequently involved the payment of money to support the centre, as well as the exemptions from episcopal control. For instance, efforts were made to dispense the new mendicant orders from the authority of their national bishops. Similarly, there were many other attempts at centralized control of the church by the papacy and its curia, including the hearing of appeals and the dispensation from canon law, which were later to prove so important in the beginnings of the English Reformation. It is important to note

---

5   Francis Oakley, *The Conciliarist Tradition: Constitutionalism in the Catholic Church, 1300-1870* (Oxford: Oxford University Press, 2003), p. 63.

6   See my essay, 'Cyprianus Anglicus: St Cyprian and the Future of Anglicanism', in Robert Hannaford (ed.), *The Future of Anglicanism* (Leominster: Gracewing, 1996), pp. 104–17; and *Bishops, Saints and Politics*, chapter 2.

that the clergy of the national churches frequently sided with their secular rulers against the influence of the papacy, which led to a series of bitter disputes, not least of which was over the calls for apostolic simplicity in the face of the luxury, centralisation and bureaucratization of the papacy.

The Council of Constance, which was convoked by John XXIII (usually regarded by Rome as an antipope) and the Emperor Sigismund, was one of the most important gatherings of the middle ages. Its course is complex and full of intrigue and mutual distrust and suspicion between the members of the rival factions – in March 1415 John XXIII fled the Council to try to disrupt it. And even today the authority of its different stages is still a matter of much debate.[7] But what is not contested is the fact that it was a huge gathering attended by 5 patriarchs, 33 cardinals, 47 archbishops, 145 bishops, 93 suffragan bishops, 132 abbots, 155 priors, 217 doctors of theology, 361 doctors of laws, 5,300 'simple priests and scholars', plus a host of others including apparently over 700 harlots, presumably to relieve some of the frustrations experienced by those called to a celibate priesthood.[8] The Council undoubtedly marks the high point of the movement referred to as Conciliarism.

One of the principal actors at Constance was the Chancellor of the University of Paris, the so-called 'doctor christianissimus', Jean Gerson (1363–1429). He helped persuade the Council to continue after the flight of John by preaching a sermon which shaped the outcome of the Council: he boldly asserted that the Pope's powers could be limited by 'the Church, or a general council representing it'. The Church, he went on, 'is so regulated by the direction of the Holy Spirit under authority from Christ that everyone of whatever rank,

---

7   Oakley, *The Conciliarist Tradition*, p. 260.
8   Oakley, *The Conciliarist Tradition*, p. 21.

even the papal, is obliged to hearken and obey it'.[9] Following this advice, at its fifth session held on 6 April 1415, the Council formally promulgated the decree *Haec sancta synodos* which asserted that the council,

> legitimately assembled in the holy Spirit, constituting a general council and representing the catholic church militant ... has power immediately from Christ; and that everyone of whatever state or dignity, even papal, is bound to obey it in those matters which pertain to the faith, the eradication of the said schism and the general reform of the said church of God in head and members. ... Anyone of whatever condition, state or dignity, even papal, who contumaciously refuses to obey the past or future mandates, statutes, ordinances or precepts of this sacred council or of any other legitimately assembled general council ... shall be subjected to well-deserved penance.[10]

By 1417 the Council had reached a number of successful outcomes, most important of which was the re-unification of the church under a single new Pope, who took the name of Martin V and resided in Rome. This was accompanied by the deposition of the other claimants. However, the Council also sought to establish the principle of conciliarism or synodality as a regular and normal feature of church life, seeing the council as a kind of court of appeal and final judge above

---

9   Gerson, 'Ambulate dum lucem habetis' in C. M. D. Crowder, *Unity, Heresy and reform, 1378-1460* (New York: St Martin's Press, 1977), pp. 76–82. On Gerson, see esp. Oakley, *The Conciliarist Tradition*, chapter 2; Brian Tierney, *Religion, Law and the Growth of Constitutional Thought* (Cambridge: Cambridge University Press, 1982); Louis B. Pascoe, *Jean Gerson: Principles of Church Reform* (Leiden: Brill, 1973).

10 Norman Tanner, *Decrees of the Ecumenical Councils* (London: Sheed and Ward, 1990), vol. i, p. 409.

anything else in the Church, including the Pope. While he might hold precedence among the bishops, he could not be regarded as exempt from control by a council. Thus in Session 39 of the Council of Constance, held in 1417, the Fathers decreed:

> The frequent holding of general councils is a pre-eminent means of cultivating the Lord's patrimony. It roots out the briars, thorns and thistles of heresies, errors and schisms, corrects deviations, reforms what is deformed and produces a richly fertile crop for the Lord's vineyard. Neglect of councils, on the other hand, spreads and fosters the aforesaid evils. ... We establish, enact, decree and ordain, by a perpetual edict, that general councils shall be held henceforth in the following way. The first shall follow in five years immediately after the end of this council, the second in seven years immediately after the end of the next council, and thereafter they are to be held every ten years for ever.[11]

The decrees also suggested that councils could be convoked without necessarily securing the agreement of the Pope. The ultimate unsuccessful fate of the *Frequens* decree, especially that councils be held every ten years, ought to be noted by all Anglicans.

How the decrees of the Council of Constance worked in practice is revealed most clearly in the somewhat complex and often deeply sad history of the next century or so, although the after-effect ripples on until today. The failure of conciliarism and the redirection of power both towards and away from the papacy led ultimately to the Reformation and its Catholic response. What might be described as the half-way house of

---

11 9 October 1417.

Conciliarism did not emerge triumphant. Councils proved ineffective, and could not command the widespread respect required if they were to uphold the unity of the Church against schismatics and heretics. Political conditions soon intervened which made the next council, which was held at Pavia and then Sienna from 1424, ineffectual and a hotbed of conflict between the papalists and the conciliarists. The Council at Basel (which later migrated to Italian soil) of 1431 through to 1449 again proved extraordinarily divisive – the tensions between conciliarism and papalism remained unresolved.

What emerged in the latter part of the fifteenth century was what has sometimes been regarded as 'the triumph of the papal monarchy',[12] at least south of the Alps. While conciliarism influenced the development of secular constitutionalism, sometimes explicitly and often profoundly,[13] its effects in the Church were rather more ambiguous. Figgis regarded the Council of Constance as a world-historical event because it prepared the ground for the sort of constitutionalism that developed in secular politics,[14] and certainly not for its influence in the Church. Where conciliarism survived in the Church it did so only as what has been called a 'counter memory', frequently suppressed by the official historians and theologians of the Church.[15] And occasionally it was simply a

---

12 Oakley, *The Conciliarist Tradition*, p. 51.
13 For an assessment of Figgis's *Gerson to Grotius*, see Francis Oakley, 'Figgis, Constance and the Divines of Paris', in *American Historical Review* 75 (1969), pp. 368–86. Oakley concludes that Figgis was right in his assessment of the Council of Constance as the turning point between medieval and modern politics (p. 386).
14 Figgis, pp. 46–8. Oakley, *The Conciliarist Tradition*, chapter 6.
15 Oakley, *The Conciliarist Tradition*, p. 7. See also p. 58 and p. 262: 'On the repression of memory and the pursuit of the politics of oblivion, after all, recent generations can certainly claim to have written the book.'

cipher for the assertion of national autonomy against Rome.[16] In the years after Constance there was a double movement in the churches. On the one hand, there was a revival of papal absolutism over the rights and claims of the national churches – the plenitude of power was re-asserted with a vengeance. On the other hand, there was also an increase in the power of the secular rulers over the churches within their states. Indeed much papal power was 'nationalized' by the nascent states of Europe. As Oakley puts it:

> The disarray and confusion in Church government engendered by the schism constituted a critical phase ... in the disintegration of what had become under papal leadership and government a genuinely international Church into congeries of what were, *de facto* if not *de jure*, national and territorial churches dominated by kings, princes, and the rulers of such proud city states as Florence and Venice.[17]

Pope Eugenius IV was willing to collude with the secular rulers, provided that they were prepared to give up on the conciliar idea. This meant that the assertion of papal power was often accompanied, perhaps ironically, by an increase in power over the Church by the prince. Indeed, it is not difficult to see in the failure of conciliarism the prehistory of the sorts of claims made by Henry VIII over the Church with his assertion of absolute imperial authority over both church and state in the Act of Supremacy of 1534.

At the same time, the sort of singular authority which emerged in the nation states was eventually also claimed by the Pope, particularly in the battles against the national churches at the Reformation. His primacy and plenitude of

---

16 Oakley, *The Conciliarist Tradition*, p. 54.
17 Oakley, *The Conciliarist Tradition*, p. 52.

power were magnified through the centuries following the collapse of conciliarism and the dismemberment of western Christianity. It would be impossible to chart the rise of papal authority from the period of Trent until twentieth century, but it is not implausible to suggest that the first Vatican Council of 1870 was the logical culmination of the anti-conciliar movement with its assertion of the rights of the Pope to make decrees independently of the rest of the Church. During the discussions, Cardinal Guidi argued that it would be anathema for the Pope to speak independently of the Church and the 'counsel of the bishops who show the tradition of their churches'. In what is apparently an authentic remark, a furious Pope Pius IX is reported to have said that this was wrong because 'I, I am the tradition. I, I am the Church!'[18] While outdoing Figgis in his rhetoric, the angry Pope was not altogether inaccurate in his understandings of his own claims to power. It was also hardly surprising that the great German Church historian Ignaz von Döllinger, who refused to accept the decrees of the Vatican Council, could claim that there was a 'profound hatred, at the bottom of the soul of every genuine ultramontane of free institutions and the whole conciliar system'.[19] Constitutionalism and liberty of any kind were threatened by papal (or any other form of) absolutism.

Conciliarism and Anglicanism

Conciliarism was thus a complex phenomenon with many consequences, some of them quite unexpected. Papal infallibility and parliamentary democracy mark two quite different trajectories emanating from the same historical

---

18   Owen Chadwick, *A History of the Popes, 1830-1914* (Oxford: Clarendon Press, 1998), pp. 210–11. For the development of papal power in the twentieth century see also Oakley, p. 261.

19   Cited in Oakley, *The Conciliarist Tradition*, p. 220.

phenomenon. Thus, although it may have been a dull period of history, this was at the same time a world-shaking dullness. What seems important in the current debates in the Anglican Communion is to locate the contemporary demands for something approaching a form of conciliarism within this broader historical context.[20] At the same time, the specific context of the development of Anglicanism in the nationalist reaction to conciliarism needs to be taken into account. Although there is no space to rehearse the history of the English Reformation, what is crucial to note in relation to the structures of the Church is that there was no possibility of any form of international conciliarism within the Church of England. The English Church under the English King was complete in itself – while it might share much with other churches (and there continued to be significant interplay between the English and the Continental churches) the whole thrust of the reforms of Henry and Elizabeth was towards self-sufficiency in the English Church. While there was significant disagreement about the relative degree of power that might be accorded to the different insitutions of church and state, virtually all Reformers were clear that power and authority resided purely within the national church and nowhere else. There was consequently something consistent about the Prayer Book teaching on General Councils. There was no automatic character to them as envisaged at Constance. Instead

> they may not be gathered together without the commandment and will of Princes. And when they be gathered together, (forasmuch as they be an assembly of men, whereof all be not governed with the Spirit and Word of God,) they may err, and sometimes have

---

20 See most recently, Paul Avis, *Beyond the Reformation? Authority, Primacy and the Unity of the Conciliar Tradition* (London: T & T Clark, 2006).

erred, even in things pertaining unto God. Wherefore things ordained by them as necessary to salvation have neither strength nor authority, unless it may be declared that they be taken out of holy Scripture.[21]

Decisions of councils were thus not supreme except when tested against Scripture – who did the declaring is left unsaid.

The end of conciliarism meant that the Church had failed to reform itself. This consequently made it necessary for the English Church to take unilateral action. In a fascinating passage which draws on the writings of Gerson, William Laud, Archbishop of Canterbury from 1633 to 1645, claimed that Gerson 'will not deny but that the Church may be reformed in parts; and that this is necessary, and that to effect it, Provincial Councils may suffice; and in some things, Diocesan'.[22] Laud then goes on to point to the right of provincial councils to 'decree in causes of faith, and in cases of reformation, where corruptions have crept into the sacraments of Christ' and then lists a number of provincial councils which have acted on their own authority.[23] Among them he includes the famous Council of Carthage (251–55) which condemned rebaptism. He concludes by asking the question: 'if this were practised so often, and in so many places, why may not a National Council of the Church of England do the like? – as she did'.[24] While Laud approved of local synods or councils (and for many at the time parliament was understood as a kind of (predominantly lay) synod), what was conspicuously absent was an international forum. The form of medieval conciliarism exhibited at Constance proved quite impossible to uphold.

---

21 Article XXI.
22 Cited in William Laud, *The Works of William Laud* (Library of Anglo-Catholic Theology) (Oxford: Parker, 1849), vol. ii, p. 170.
23 Laud, *Works*, ii, p. 171.
24 Laud, *Works*, ii, p. 172.

Again without going into historical detail,[25] I think it would be fair to characterize the development of Anglicanism as the planting of this national church ideal in the many varied parts of the world where the influence of England reached. For instance, political realities forced this on the Amercian Church after the Revolution. It became wholly independent from its mother Church – indeed it could not be said to have been 'in full communion' with the Church of England until 1840 when American clergy were first allowed to minister in England. The planting of colonial and missionary churches followed a similar pattern – churches rapidly became self-governing, retaining the national church ideal, even when they co-existed alongside other denominations. Even the word 'Anglican' means nothing more than 'English'. If this term is to be applied to non-English churches it can refer to little more than the governing ideal of the English Church – that is, ecclesiastical independence. The idea of a worldwide forum for Anglicanism, which was begun extremely tentatively in 1867 by Archbishop Longley after pressure from a number of quarters, proved impossible for his fellow Archbishop of York. The status and authority of such a forum remained (and to some extent remain) unclear.

The international ideal was not the guiding principle of Anglicanism – even the so-called Chicago-Lambeth quadrilateral of 1888, which remains one of the key statements of what it might be to be an Anglican, was initially based on internal American efforts to re-unite the Church after the divisions of the Civil War. It was adopted as a relatively uncontroversial statement about what constituted Anglican identity – Bible, creeds, the sacraments of baptism and communion, and bishops. On the whole, there was remarkably little reflection on what it was to be an Anglican. While

---

25 See my *Anglicanism: A Very Short Introduction* (Oxford: Oxford University Press, 2006), chapters 6 and 7.

national churches were often divided over the teachings of the different ecclesiastical parties, it would be fair to say that Anglican ecclesiology was as underdeveloped as was catholic ecclesiology in the early middle ages. Ecclesiology, one might suggest, is a response to need – where there was little major division and few international problems there was little need for reflection on the nature of the worldwide church. For most people Article XIX of the Thirty-nine Articles was probably sufficient: 'The visible Church of Christ is a congregation of faithful men, in the which the pure Word of God is preached, and the Sacraments be duly ministered according to Christ's ordinance in all those things that of necessity are requisite to the same.' The local predominated over the universal in the Church of England's self-definition (translated from Article VII of the Augsburg Confession).

Occasional schism and division made an international forum useful – and here one can draw on the example of the Colenso controversy which was a good illustration of the problems encountered in non-Western cultures, in his case that of polygamy, coupled with his attachment to liberal biblical scholarship. As the Lambeth Conference developed it began to carry moral authority and weight. The collection of bishops from across the world was able to discuss and debate issues and write encyclical letters of surprisingly good quality. Yet it did not become the equivalent of a medieval council – the bishops gathered together claimed no power, in the sense of legally enforceable sanctions, but merely a persuasive authority based mainly on their office and some sort of shared ethos and history. Where Constance could (and did) behead heretics and depose popes, Lambeth could simply suggest to the participating bishops that decapitation might be a useful and sensible solution to a particular problem, and the local churches would be left to execute the judgement. And the other so-called instruments of unity, the Anglican Consultative Council, the Primates' Meeting, as well as the Archbishop of

Canterbury himself, have no more authority than the Lambeth Conference – there is no Anglican Communion canon law, except when national churches choose to accept the laws of other provinces. Given the primitive status of these international bodies, it is hardly surprising that serious division in the Anglican Communion is provoking more concerted theological reflection on the nature of Anglicanism and the ways in which it deals with issues arising between the national churches.

Conclusion

Historical parallels are not usually too helpful. But sometimes they can assist us in pointing to the complexities of issues. It may be of some use for the contemporary church to remind it that international ecclesial problem-solving without a centralized system of control and power was not successful in the fifteenth century. While the papacy might have been united at Constance, the conciliar principle was soon repressed and ousted by the double alternative of national churches or a centralized papacy. Anglican churches stemmed from the national churches which reached their climax in the Reformation. Yet in recent years significant dispute and schism has emerged between and within these national churches which comprise the Anglican Communion – the international bonds, many of which carry with them significant exchanges of money and personnel, are under threat. Some churches have acted according to the venerable principle of national (or in the jargon of Anglicanism, 'provincial') autonomy and have taken novel and controversial actions. This has led to the occasional accusation of heresy and threat of excommunication or schism. Sometimes these threats have been put into practice, as has recently happened in Tanzania where the House of Bishops has declared 'that henceforth the Anglican Church of Tanzania shall not knowingly accept financial and material aid from Dioceses, parishes, Bishops, priests, individuals and institutions in the Episcopal Church (USA) that condone homosexual practice or bless same sex unions'.[26]

The Windsor Report was commissioned by the Archbishop of Canterbury following the election of Gene Robinson to the Diocese of New Hampshire in 2003, and the provision for blessing of same-sex couples in the Canadian diocese of New Westminster. It recommended the creation of a Covenant which was intended to provide a more coherent basis for Anglican identity, and would be accompanied with a number of legal sanctions which would be adopted into the laws of the national churches.[27] More recently the Joint Standing Committee of the Anglican Communion has produced a detailed consideration of what is required in a Covenant. This document has already provoked a large number of responses.[28] It is still uncertain what will happen and precisely what form the Covenant will take, or even whether it will see the light of day at all. It could contain a strong doctrinal confession which would make the Anglican Communion into something approaching a confessional church along the lines of Lutheranism. Some influential voices are calling for legal sanctions, which would certainly give a different feel to the status and authority of the central institutions of Anglicanism. However, this change of status is something that can already be perceived in the ways in which the Resolution of the 1998 Lambeth Conference that homosexual practice is

---

26 12 December 2006 posted at
http://www.anglicancommunion.org/acns/articles/42/25/acns4227.cfm
27 *TWR*, Appendix 2.
28 Joint Standing Committee, *Towards an Anglican Covenant: A Consultation Paper on the Covenant Proposal of the Windsor Report* (London: Anglican Communion Office, 2006).

'incompatible with Scripture' (1.10) has been received and elevated into something far more than simply a piece of moral advice. Similarly, the style of argumentation in both reports tends to be founded on the self-referential use of Anglican Communion texts understood as some kind of dogmatic rulings akin to statute law, rather than a serious appraisal of the breadth of the Christian tradition through history. The status of the instruments of unity has thus gradually increased.

In all this, it seems to me that there is perhaps something to be learnt from Constance. It solved a particular problem once and for all – from that time, except for the ten year pontificate of the antipope Felix V from 1439–49, there has been only one Pope. Nevertheless conciliarism was not successful in its wider purpose of trying to provide a final court of appeal beyond even the curia and the papacy. The reasons for this seem quite clear – Popes clamoured for clear and unambiguous lines of control, but, more importantly, so too did national rulers. Princes and their churches were content with a much looser international structure, or no international structure at all, which culminated on the one side with Gallicanism and on the other with the Reformation. It is feasible that the claims made by Constance in its decree *Haec Sancta* were simply too immodest and impractical to work. It went further than was required, threatening the power brokers of medieval Europe. Nevertheless it offered a constitution, and, although it was far from democratic, it embraced something of the principles of nationalism (in that voting was by nations) and representation (in that various constituencies were represented).[29] That said, the conciliar solution to an occasional schism was very different from the institutionalization of conciliarism.

The dangers are that an Anglican Covenant could go too far – and this could result in some sort of rather messy new

---

29 See Hans Küng, *Structures of the Church* (New York: Nelson, 1964), pp. 270–84.

reformation. The first lesson to be learnt from Constance is not to be too ambitious. It would be easy for national churches, or at least significant minorities within them, simply to opt out and withdraw from the Anglican Communion altogether (the analogy would be with the antipopes). Indeed, many Anglicans might well prefer other identities if competing expressions of Anglicanism no longer offer what they regard as orthodoxy. Despite these dangers, however, I would suggest that it is important that something of the conciliar ideal be retained – after all it offers a way of addressing particular issues and has occasionally met with a degree of success. But I would also counsel the virtues of what Figgis called a 'tepid constitutionalism'. Tepid things, like grey things, are seldom accorded the highest respect, but there is something to be said for working towards a form of conciliarism which promotes open conversation, dialogue, respect and a recognition that there can be quite a radical measure of disagreement among those committed to Jesus Christ. If Anglicans want to remain together it would be sensible to encourage that desire through a modest form of 'tepid' constitutionalism. But if they don't want to, then no amount of constitutionalism will succeed in holding the churches together, so it might be better avoided altogether. The failure of conciliarism shows clearly that it is not necessary to hold a council every ten years for churches to survive. If the constitutionalism gets too hot then reaction against it might dismember the Church altogether – there is a rather dull precedent and we are still living with the consequences.

4

The Episcopal Church in the USA and the Covenant: The Place of the Chicago-Lambeth Quadrilateral

R. WILLIAM FRANKLIN

This chapter introduces the topic of the Episcopal Church in the United States of America and the proposed Anglican Covenant, with special reference to the Chicago-Lambeth Quadrilateral. First, I consider the place of the Covenant in the report of the Special Commission on the Episcopal Church and the Anglican Communion of 2006, as well as the treatment of the concept of an Anglican Covenant in the Resolutions of the 75th General Convention of the Episcopal Church during the summer of 2006. I then go on to discuss what the history of the Chicago-Lambeth Quadrilateral of 1886–88 may contribute to our understanding of previous covenant processes, and the role theology has played in such considerations in the Anglican Communion over the past century.

The Special Commission on the Episcopal Church and the Anglican Communion was constituted in late 2005 by the Presiding Bishop, Frank Griswold to assist the 75th General Convention in considering recent developments in the American Episcopal Church and the Anglican Communion, with a view toward maintaining the highest degree of communion possible. The Special Commission met five times between November 2005 and March 2006, and it presented its findings to the 75th General Convention in Columbus, Ohio in June 2006. Among the fourteen members of the Commission were the new Presiding Bishop and Primate of the Episcopal Church, the Most Reverend Katharine Jefferts Schori, and one of the US members of the new Covenant Design Group, Prof. Katherine Grieb, of the Virginia Theological Seminary.

Following the release of *The Windsor Report* in October 2004, the House of Bishops of the Episcopal Church, in their meeting of March 2005, adopted their own 'Covenant Statement' that offered a 'provisional measure to contribute to a time of healing and for the educational process called for in the Windsor Report'.[1] This 2005 Covenant reaffirmed the bishops' commitment to the Chicago-Lambeth Quadrilateral, and their earnest desire to remain in full communion with the Archbishop of Canterbury and the other Churches of the Anglican Communion. Section VI of the Report of the Special Commission in 2006 was the logical next step for the Episcopal Church's consideration of an Anglican Covenant. In the recent history of the Episcopal Church, covenants have been useful to help clarify the nature of relationships in service to God's mission, both in inter-Anglican relations and ecumenically. Covenants with recently autonomous provinces of the Anglican Communion, that have formerly been missionary dioceses of the Episcopal Church – including Liberia, the Philippines, Mexico, Central America, and a new proposal for Brazil – have spelled out the nature of mutual responsibility and interdependence in the Body of Christ. In the light of a long history of creating and affirming covenants, the Special Commission made the following recommendation to the General Convention:

---

1 'A Covenant Statement of the House of Bishops' (New York: Episcopal News Service, 15 March 2005), §3.

Nourished by Scripture and the sacraments, and sharing a common faith with sisters and brothers in Christ around the world, we trust that the Episcopal Church will want to participate in the covenant conversations across the Communion. The Special Commission embraces the processes leading up to the development of an Anglican Covenant as part of our commitment to interdependence and common service to God's mission.[2]

Subsequently, in late June 2006, the 75th General Convention passed Resolution A166 entitled 'Anglican Covenant Development Process' including these words which resolved that

the 75th General Convention of the Episcopal Church, as a demonstration of our commitment to mutual responsibility and interdependence in the Anglican Communion, supports the process of the development of an Anglican Covenant that underscores our unity in faith, order, and common life in the service of God's mission.[3]

This resolution was very clear. It supports the creation of an Anglican Covenant as suggested by *The Windsor Report*, the Primates' Meeting of February 2005, and the 13th Meeting of the Anglican Consultative Council. It directs appropriate bodies in the Episcopal Church to serve as resources for the

---

2   *One Baptism, One Hope in God's Call: The Report of the Special Commission on the Episcopal Church and the Anglican Communion* (New York: Episcopal Church Center, 2006), p. 25.

3   *Resolutions of the 75th General Convention of the Episcopal Church* (New York: Episcopal Church Center, 2006), §A166; also at: http://www.episcopalchurch.org/gc2006.org/legislation/

development of such a covenant, and to report to the Episcopal Church regularly as to the current covenant proposals that may emerge.

But what sort of covenant would be acceptable to the Episcopal Church? The Chicago-Lambeth Quadrilateral clearly seems to be a model for a Covenant which would fit the characteristics of an acceptable document, the sort of document outlined in the report of the Special Commission. The Report of the Commission concludes with these words:

> Both the Episcopal Church and the bishops of the Anglican Communion encourage and recognize a diversity of theological opinions within the Christian Church subject to the broad boundaries defined by the Chicago-Lambeth Quadrilateral, as quoted, which has been a guiding principle in the relations of the Episcopal Church since 1886. The Quadrilateral's generosity of spirit has fostered cooperative service to the mission of Christ both around the world and at home. For the sake of that same mission, our generosity toward those within our tradition should be at least as great as toward those of other traditions.[4]

The report of the Special Commission cites paragraph 9 of the Anglican Primates' 'Dromantine Statement', also referenced as footnote two of the Joint Standing Committee's *Towards an Anglican Covenant*, as providing support for proposing the Quadrilateral as one model for what an Anglican Covenant might look like. The Primates at Dromantine noted:

---

4   *Report of the Special Commission*, p. 33.

We were glad to be reminded of the extensive precedents for covenants that many Anglican churches have established with ecumenical partners, and that even within our Communion the Chicago/Lambeth Quadrilateral has already been effectively operating as a form of covenant that secures our basic commitment to scripture, the Nicene Creed, the two Sacraments of the Gospel and the Historic Episcopate. We therefore commend this proposal as a project that should be given further consideration in the Provinces of the Communion between now and the Lambeth Conference of 2008.[5]

But there are also questions and severe reservations about the suitability of the Chicago-Lambeth Quadrilateral to serve as a form of covenant adequate to the interdependent life of the Communion in the twenty-first century. The Joint Standing Committee's *Towards an Anglican Covenant*, goes on to say:

Considerable thought has to be given to the form of the covenant which is needed in the life of the Communion at the present time. Does it need to be short, rather like the Bonn Agreement, or complex? The content could simply restate a lapidary Anglican formula (such as the Lambeth-Chicago Quadrilateral). If so, then although the process leading to its adoption will be of very great educational importance and symbolic significance, it will have limited impact on

---

5 'Dromantine Statement', §9; cited in Joint Standing Committee, *Towards an Anglican Covenant: A Consultation Paper on the Covenant Proposal of the Windsor Report* (London: The Anglican Communion Office, 2006), p. 1.

the internal structures of the Churches and Provinces, or on their relationship in legal terms with one another. Most Churches and Provinces should have little difficulty in signing up to such a Covenant, so long as the text confines itself to widely-established and respected principles.[6]

And the views contained in this paragraph certainly hold true for the Episcopal Church. The General Convention in the summer of 2006 made it very clear in its resolution 'that it should have little difficulty in signing up to such a covenant'. [7] But some Episcopalians see the Quadrilateral as not going far enough. In an essay of 2004 on 'The Windsor Report and the American Evasion of Communion', Ephraim Radner, the second United States member of the Covenant Design Group, comments on the suitability of the Quadrilateral as a model for the Covenant:

> [Robert] Hughes [an American professor of theology at the University of the South] – along with many others – uses the Quadrilateral as a guide here: the fact that the Quadrilateral describes the Creeds as a 'sufficient statement of faith' makes them the only element that is 'essential,' and therefore subject, in their referents, to external judgment in cases where a church somehow undermines their authority. Everything else (including teaching on and standards of 'morals') belongs wholly to the sphere of autonomous local definition and discernment. (This is the kind of standard used in the Righter Trial decision,

---

6   *Towards an Anglican Covenant*, pp. 4–5.
7   Resolution A166: Anglican Covenant.

which distinguished between 'core doctrine' and 'morals'.)

It is important to see what the practical payoff for this kind of boundary-setting is. Apart from Creeds, Hughes has constructed an arena wherein there is no need among churches to reach 'consensus' about any matter at all, since all non-creedal disputes are over matters that are, in fact, nonessential. Local autonomy is granted a far-ranging sphere of action. ...

It is possible that Hughes believes that the Quadrilateral itself provides the definitions we need for this. But such a use of the Quadrilateral is internally incoherent (not to say historically misapplied, as to its stated purpose for the sake of ecumenical discussion). If the Creeds were 'sufficient' in terms of a defining the 'boundaries of essence' exhaustively, there would be no Quadrilateral at all: Creeds do not mention Scripture, Eucharist, or Historical Episcopate, all of which the Quadrilateral makes essential in its 'sacred deposit.' But if we accept these other elements as defining 'essence,' where do they come from, and what does their origin say about the character of 'doctrinal, disciplinary, and liturgical essence' itself?[8]

I propose to respond in this chapter to Radner's questions posed in this 2004 essay, since they will inevitably emerge again within the Covenant Design Group, as the draft Covenant is revised in time for the Lambeth Conference in 2008. I propose to respond by answering another set of

---

8   Ephraim Radner, 'The Windsor Report and the American Evasion of Communion' (The Anglican Communion Institute, December 2004), pp. 4–5 at:
     http://www.AnglicanCommunioninstitute.org/articles/
     American_Evasion_of Communion.htm

questions which place the issue of covenant within the history of the Anglican Communion over the last century and a half. The questions which I think are now important for the Episcopal Church to ask as it contemplates participating in the Covenant process are these: where did the Quadrilateral come from? What does it say about the Episcopal Church's understanding of the doctrinal, disciplinary, and liturgical essence of Anglicanism, particularly as they are thought of at the international level, and what are the historical precedents for the allegiance of the Episcopal Church to theological articles of faith that might serve in some way as an international covenant? What is the heritage of the Episcopal Church as to its international role and international links in full communion, and how might the safeguarding of those links to the larger Anglican Communion be related to the history and the evolution of the Chicago-Lambeth Quadrilateral?

The Chicago-Lambeth Quadrilateral

When the Chicago Quadrilateral of 1886 was received by the Lambeth Conference in 1888 and restated with some modifications by that Conference, something unprecedented and unparalleled happened. For the first time one of the great branches within Christianity adopted for its own greater internal unity, and for the orientation of the endeavours toward a greater church unity generally, a short, definitive formula of belief. Although, because the nature of the Lambeth Conferences, the decision of 1888 was not canonically binding upon Anglicanism, it has been one of the most effective and enduring actions ever taken in the history of the Conferences. Subsequent Lambeth Conferences have either quoted the Quadrilateral again or have referred to its basic and guiding character. In the Episcopal Church the Chicago-

Lambeth Quadrilateral is indeed regarded as a binding standard, a position restated in the resolutions of the last General Convention of the summer of 2006.[9] I could cite many more examples of several forms of 'reception' of the Quadrilateral in many Provinces of the Anglican Communion as the binding standard within Anglicanism, and this reception has effectively shaped also the Anglican position in every one of our ecumenical encounters for over one hundred and forty years: in the Faith and Order Movement, in church union negotiations, and in the bilateral dialogues.

The Quadrilateral emerged in the United States of America. In the United States we encounter in the nineteenth century an enormous zeal and enthusiasm for shaping and strengthening the unity and identity of our still young nation, which was, in the second half of the century, desperately struggling to heal the wounds of the Civil War of 1861 to 1865. In this situation the Churches, too, began to take seriously their unparalleled divisions and fragmentations. Methodists, Baptists, and Presbyterians had divided into Northern and Southern churches over the issue of slavery. The Episcopalians were severely fragmented into networks of Evangelical and Anglo-Catholic dioceses, which, after the bloody divisions of the Civil War, were seen now to render a narrow counter-witness to the general spirit and aspirations of the time. Discovering the responsibility of the churches for the nation as a whole, where there was no established national church, many began to develop a great number of diverse efforts for unity both within the denominations and across the denominational divides, including within the Episcopal Church.

During the American Civil War William Reed Huntington was Rector of the Episcopal parish of All Saints in the bustling

---

9   'Resolution A169: Amend Canon III.1: Quadrilateral and Exercise
     of Ministry', in *Resolutions of General Convention*, §A169.

industrial city of Worcester, Massachusetts. In 1883 he became Rector of Grace Church in New York City, which was then the most fashionable Episcopal Church in the United States. The opulent wedding scene of Edith Wharton's *The Age of Innocence* takes place in Grace Church, and Wharton describes a thinly disguised Huntington as the epitome of the fashionable American rector. Out of the sacrifices of the Civil War and the example set by Abraham Lincoln, Huntington was drawn to Christian work for greater human unity. In New York City he became part of a circle of prominent Episcopalian internationalists, including J. P. Morgan, who were founders of the American Episcopal churches in Rome, Florence, and Paris, and also of the American Academy in Rome. Huntington was a delegate to thirteen General Conventions of the Episcopal Church, and key to the building of the Cathedral Church of Saint John the Divine on Morningside Heights in Manhattan. In 1870, in his *The Church-Idea: An Essay towards Unity*,[10] Huntington developed the Anglican concept of a visible, organic unity. Huntington's 'church-idea' was adopted overwhelmingly by the American House of Bishops at Chicago, Illinois, on 20 October 1886, and for this reason it became known as the 'Chicago Quadrilateral'.

The centre of Huntington's concept is the 'Anglican principle', to be distinguished from the 'Anglican system', which principle, Huntington believed, is continuous with the standards of the early church and comes to expression in the four points of the 'Quadrilateral of pure Anglicanism'. These four points are the acceptance of the Holy Scriptures as the Word of God, the primitive creeds as the rule of faith, the two sacraments ordained by Christ Himself, and the episcopate as

---

10   William Reed Huntington, *The Church-Idea: An Essay Towards Unity* (First Edition, New York: E. P. Dutton, 1870).

the key-stone of governmental unity. Within these four points Huntington believed that the 'Church of the Reconciliation may stand secure'.[11] The goal of Huntington's scheme is a united national church which is able to reflect the unity of the new nation and to fulfil, with the joint forces of all the parties of the Episcopal Church and of other denominations, its function and responsibility within the public, social life of the United States. Huntington believed that a further purpose of the Quadrilateral was to move the Episcopal Church from its isolated, withdrawn, privileged status within American society, and among the denominations, and thrust it forward towards greater visibility, public responsibility, and full communion with other Christians. At the end of his *The Church-Idea*, Huntington has these words:

> If our whole ambition as Anglicans in America be to continue a small, but eminently respectable body of Christians, and to offer a refuge to people of refinement and sensibility, who are shocked by the irreverences they are apt to encounter elsewhere; in a word, if we care to be only a countercheck and not a force in society; then let us say as much in plain terms, and frankly renounce any and all claim to Catholicity. We have only, in such a case, to wrap the robe of our dignity about us, and walk quietly along in a seclusion no one will take much trouble to disturb. Thus may we be a Church in name, and a sect in deed.
>
> But if we aim at something nobler than this, if we would have our Communion become national in very

---

11 Cited in J. Robert Wright, 'Heritage and Vision: The Chicago-Lambeth Quadrilateral', in J. Robert Wright (ed.), *Quadrilateral at One Hundred* (Cincinnati, OH: Forward Movement Publications, 1988), p. 10.

truth, – in other words, if we would bring the Church of Christ into the closest possible sympathy with the throbbing, sorrowing, sinning, repenting, aspiring heart of this great people, – then let us press our reasonable claims to be the reconciler of a divided household, not in a spirit of arrogance (which ill befits those whose best possessions have come to them by inheritance), but with affectionate earnestness and an intelligent zeal.[12]

Huntington spoke of a new grasp of the universality of the Church as displacing the American obsession with national election, of the belief in the 'manifest destiny' of the American people. He wanted to go beyond the nation as the only construct of the Church, beyond any notion of a provincial Catholicism, which be believed was an American contradiction in terms. For Huntington, the Church is and shall be a universal society, and for this reason he saw that the purpose of the Quadrilateral was to move the Episcopal Church beyond its sectarian, nineteenth-century provincialism. The Church, in Huntington's view, is a new select society brought into being by Jesus, in the sense that because of Him it is embodied and made visible. The Church, as in the view of the English nineteenth-century theologian Frederick Denison Maurice (and Huntington was directly influenced by Maurice's *The Kingdom of Christ* of 1838), the Church is a universal society encompassing all of humankind. Huntington spoke of the Church as beginning with a family, progressing to a nation, and coming to full revelation only in the universal kingdom proclaimed by Jesus and sustained by the Holy Spirit. And so a second purpose of the Quadrilateral was to move Anglicanism across the globe beyond what he perceived to be the cultural

---

12   Cited in Robert Wright, 'Heritage and Vision', p. 45.

constraints placed upon it and derived from the Church of England. So when we read *The Church-Idea* of 1870 today in the light of our current debates, we are struck by these qualities through which Huntington seeks to achieve his goal of breaking out of narrow boundaries. *The Church-Idea* is, in a humorous, good-natured way, very rare in a work of Anglican theology: anti-Episcopalian, anti-British, and universalist in its proposed scheme of Christian renewal.

Even the cover of the 1870 edition of *The Church-Idea* depicts the universalism of the Church of Christ and prints the words, 'Now the coat was without seam woven from the top throughout' (Jn 19.23). Huntington likens the absolutely essential features of the Anglican position not to something Episcopalian or English, but to a feature of the Italian landscape, to the four fortress cities of Lombardy – Mantua, Verona, Peschiera, and Legnano – that had provided Austria a means to keep northern Italy under its control. This is the most famous passage of *The Church-Idea*:

> What are the essential, the absolutely essential features of the Anglican position? When it is proposed to make Anglicanism the basis of a Church of Reconciliation, it is above all things necessary to determine what Anglicanism pure and simple is. The word brings up before the eyes of some a flutter of surplices, a vision of village spires and cathedral towers, a somewhat stiff and stately company of deans, prebendaries, and choristers, and that is about all. But we greatly mistake if we imagine that the Anglican principle has no substantial existence apart from these accessories. Indeed, it is only when we have stripped Anglicanism of the picturesque costume which English life has thrown around it, that we can fairly study its anatomy, or understand its possibilities of power and adaptation.

The Anglican *principle* and the Anglican *system* are two very different things. The writer does not favor attempting to foist the whole Anglican system upon America, while yet he believes that the Anglican principle is America's best hope.

At no time since the Reformation has the Church of England been in actual fact the spiritual home of the nation. Even a majority of the people of Great Britain are to-day without her pale. Could a system which has failed to secure comprehensiveness on its native soil, hope for any larger measure of success in a strange land?

But what if it can be shown that the Anglican system has failed in just so far as it has been untrue to the Anglican principle? And what if it can be shown that here in America we have an opportunity to give that principle the only fair trial it has ever had?

The true Anglican position, like the City of God in the Apocalypse, may be said to lie foursquare. Honestly to accept that position is to accept, –

1. The Holy Scriptures as the Word of God.
2. The Primitive Creeds as the Rule of Faith.
3. The two Sacraments ordained by Christ himself.
4. The Episcopate as the key-stone of Governmental Unity.

These four points, like the four famous fortresses of Lombardy, make 'the Quadrilateral' of pure Anglicanism. Within them the Church of Reconciliation may stand secure. Because the English State-Church has muffled these first principles in a cloud of non-essentials, and has said to the people of the land, 'Take all this or nothing,' she mourns today the loss of half her children. Only by avoiding the like fatal error can the American branch of the Anglican Church hope to save herself from becoming in effect, whatever she may be in name, a sect. Only by a wise discrimination between what can and what cannot be conceded for the sake of unity, is unity attainable.[13]

The Quadrilateral stated clear theological conditions for establishing even partial and imperfect communion. It provided a theological structure which might make possible a discussion at the international level. There was close to a common theology of ordination held among the Episcopal Church's House of Bishops who had adopted Huntington's four points in Chicago in 1886. Almost all believed ordination by a bishop in due succession to be a sacramental action and confirmation to be an apostolic rite. All believed the proposition that the Bible is indispensable to the Church. The two great classical creeds were easily supported by all. Biblical authority underpinned the theological affirmation of the necessity of baptism and the eucharist, a proposition to which no one dissented.

Similarly the clause of the Quadrilateral adopted at the Lambeth Conference in 1888 concerning the episcopate asks all to assert that this order is 'historic', a proposition that no one denied either at Chicago in 1886 or at Lambeth in 1888. All held that the episcopal order has been around for a very long time, is attested to in the New Testament itself, and no one objected when it was implied that this was the sole position of Anglicanism, from which it had never shifted.

The four points of the Quadrilateral, though they may be said to be institutional, do contain a theological perspective, though neither the Chicago nor the Lambeth forms of the

---

13   Huntington, *The Church-Idea*, pp. 155–7.

Quadrilateral make any elaborate theological expansion of the four items. The four points are put forth in the shortest possible form, seeking to win the widest possible adherence, but they are not for this reason devoid of theological content. Without a doubt, the bishops of the Anglican Communion in 1888, and leaders of the other Christian Churches, were being invited to accept the catholic tradition in this new articulation, without an expanded commentary of doctrinal tradition, but the elements of the catholic tradition are there nonetheless, and these facts are asserted to be the norm for life in communion.

The focus, then, of the Quadrilateral, is upon a series of things: Holy Scripture, the creeds, the two sacraments, and the historic episcopate. In each case the Quadrilateral also qualifies the noun which names each of the four points with a further phrase which explains how these nouns are to be understood theologically. For example, the creed is to be understood as 'the sufficient statement of the Christian faith'. In an essay on how these 'things' formed the theological foundation of full communion in the nineteenth century for the Anglican Communion, Gillian Evans comments on the evolution of Anglican theology which is taking place in the formulation of the Quadrilateral:

> The difference is crucial. And so, of any one of the Thirty-Nine Articles, I may say, 'I believe that ...,' and make by quoting it a propositional statement of my doctrinal position on the issue in question. But of any one of the clauses of the Lambeth Quadrilateral, I must say, 'I believe in ... .'
>
> When the bishops of Lambeth in 1888 called the clauses of the Quadrilateral 'articles' they no doubt had it in mind to draw a parallel with the word 'article' as used in the Thirty-Nine Articles. ... The intended connotation is clear. The Quadrilateral clauses are to

'supply a basis.' An 'article' is envisioned as something indisputable among Anglicans, a rock on which one may build. ... As a result, the Lambeth bishops seem to have used the word 'article' for something which could have been called a *locus communis*. ... Lambeth 1888 says, 'the following articles supply a basis'.[14]

So this nineteenth-century formulation produced in the United States seemed to offer to worldwide Anglicanism terms of reconciliation which are clear theological boundaries for life in communion. To say that there is no precedent for a covenant which provides for such a definition of what is necessary to be in full communion with the Anglican Churches is to overlook the place of the Quadrilateral within Anglican history. Against this backcloth, we can, amidst the Communion's circumstances of today, more easily understand why this American text, forged out of the national trauma of the American Civil War, offered to the Lambeth Conference of 1888 a programmatic formula that seemed to offer hope and match the times, and may be interpreted as a precedent for the Covenant being called for in the twenty-first century.

Bishop William Stevens Perry, Episcopal Bishop of Iowa, was a leading thinker in the Episcopal Church in the nineteenth century. He was a member of the House of Bishops at Chicago in 1886 and also present at Lambeth in 1888. His analysis of what Chicago and Lambeth meant by using the term 'the Historic Episcopate' is evidence that an American participant understood the Quadrilateral to contain theological content. He wrote:

---

14 Gilliam R. Evans, 'Permanence in the Revealed Truth and Continuous Exploration of its Meaning', in Wright, *Quadrilateral at One Hundred*, pp. 115, 114.

That any theory or definition of the Historic Episcopate was intended by the American Bishops inconsistent with the call of God to all nations and to all peoples to *the unity of His Church*, is certainly untenable. That there was a Church – the Church of Christ, existing, visible, militant, upon the earth – was the belief of the great majority of the Bishops assembled at Chicago in 1886, if it was not the conviction of every member of this body. That the Historic Episcopate existed in direct, continuous succession from the Apostles' times ... was indisputably the conviction of every Bishop at Chicago and, we are confident, of every Bishop at Lambeth, with possibly two or three exceptions. That to this Church thus constituted, thus 'built upon the foundation of the Apostles and Prophets, Jesus Christ Himself being the chief corner-stone,' was promised the presence of its Lord and Master for all time to come, ... we believe to be the conviction of every Bishop in the world. That for the return to unity of those long separated and estranged, – schismatics in fact, though often not in intent or even in guilt, – the Historic Episcopate, confessedly flexible in its administration, might be adapted to varied circumstances, even to the provision of a Bishop for every large centre of population, ... this adaptation or accommodation of the Historic Episcopate might effect the longed-for return to unity, – this was the wish, the purpose, the prayer of the great body of the Chicago and the Lambeth Bishops. Views inconsistent with this understanding of the proposition were not even breathed by any Bishop at Chicago.[15]

---

15   William Stevens Perry, *Church Reunion Discussed on the Basis of the*

The Quadrilateral was also given a theological role by the movement in the US Episcopal Church which ultimately issued in the World Conference on Faith and Order. In 1910 the General Convention of the Episcopal Church resolved that a joint Commission of the Convention be appointed to bring about a Conference for the consideration of questions touching Faith and Order. Until 1920, the responsibility for preparing such a conference lay solely in the hands of this Episcopal Church commission which communicated its intentions and considerations by means of the first numbered Faith and Order pamphlets, numbers one through thirty-two, which were distributed throughout the World, and whose model of full communion was based upon the standard of the Quadrilateral as the basis of full communion. Clearly the theology of the four points of the Quadrilateral had a considerable influence in shaping the first World Conferences on Faith and Order in 1926 and 1937, and above all in the concept of organic unity related to full communion, which is also directly referred to in the series of questions, summary reports, resolutions and drafts which were produced by the Faith and Order Conferences.

Conclusion

Through the early twentieth century the Quadrilateral served as the standard theological statement to identify issues of unity and communion within Anglicanism, as well as also to identify ecumenically significant issues, as, for example, in the Lambeth Conference of 1920 with its 'Appeal to All Christian People'. In 1920 the Quadrilateral's fourth article was reworded to declare that the visible unity of the Church

---

Lambeth Propositions of 1888, cited in Wright, Heritage and Vision, p. 19.

required 'a ministry acknowledged by every part of the Church as possessing not only the inward call of the Spirit but also the commission of Christ and the authority of the whole body'.[16] Internal theological differences within the Anglican Communion in 1920 are no doubt the prime reason for the weakness of this 'Appeal', as also of the explication of the Quadrilateral which is attached to the 'Appeal'. In 1920 the Lambeth Conference could not clothe the minimal theological statements of the Quadrilateral with much enriched content without finding that it had lost some of its own brethren among the Anglican bishops. So into the twentieth century the Quadrilateral continued to play as much of an internal role within Anglicanism, as an instrument for coherence, as it played a role as an ecumenical standard in guiding relations with those outside the Anglican Communion.

For example, in 1923 at a joint conference with Nonconformist theologians held at Lambeth Palace, the representatives of the Church of England, all but one of whom were bishops, declared that they could not declare non-episcopal ministries to be 'invalid', and that the very concept of validity was one they found unhelpful when they were dealing with an unquestionable spiritual reality. On the other hand, they immediately went on to say that even 'real ministries of Christ's Word and Sacraments' could be 'irregular or defective', and they did not regard the preface to the ordinal of 1662 as formulating merely a local rule of discipline for the Church of England, but rather as enshrining a theological principle of order that Anglicans could not break without painful consequences for the internal cohesion of the Anglican

---

16 Lambeth Conference 1920, 'Appeal to All Christian People', in Wright, 'Heritage and Vision', p. 26.

Communion.[17] They envisaged the real possibility of an internal Anglican schism if the ordinal's requirement of episcopal ordination were to be set aside or made optional. In this document of 1923 the Quadrilateral is clearly used to define, once again, theological boundaries for full communion within Anglicanism.

Though obscure, I think this 1923 text is important for our debates today, and it is a significant expression of a view, based on the emerging tradition of interpretations of the Quadrilateral, that the Anglican Communion does possess theological standards with which to treat essential matters of order, and which can be applied to the doctrines of the creed and to the use of the two sacraments of the Gospel, and to the authority of the Bible as God's Word.

And the Quadrilateral continued, through the next seventy years, to be the standard by which inclusion within the Anglican Communion was measured. The traumas of English discussions of the Quadrilateral in the 1920s had long-term effects of a lasting kind upon the shape of the Communion: upon the questions raised by the reunion scheme in South India which eventually took the Anglicans there out of full communion with the see of Canterbury, and by the reunion scheme in North India and Pakistan, whose full communion was accepted by the Lambeth Conference of 1958, after important revisions were made in the scheme. It was not until further changes had been made, based on the Quadrilateral as the standard, however, that the full communion of North India and Pakistan with Canterbury was achieved in 1972. The Quadrilateral's implied theology of holy orders was the framework for all of this discussion.

---

17 Henry Chadwick, 'The Quadrilateral in England', in Wright, *Quadrilateral at One Hundred*, p. 149.

Until the end of the twentieth century, the Quadrilateral remained the theological cornerstone by which the Episcopal Church and most of the Provinces of the Anglican Communion approached the question of what was required for full communion with other Anglican Provinces. William Reed Huntington, in his first proposal of the Quadrilateral in 1870, had advocated a broad inclusiveness, responsible scholarship, balanced moderation, concentration upon essentials, and generosity of interpretation, which influenced the thought and action of many within his own American Church, and beyond it.

Huntington's brief formula, though imperfect and reductionist in many respects, was clearly a short theological covenant, and because of its theological content, it has been the most effective text in the nineteenth and twentieth centuries, as a carrier of and a continuing pointer to a broader vision to be received by others by means of modification, expansion, and application in specific historical moments and contexts. I believe this should now be the next step of the Covenant Design Group: to adhere to the Quadrilateral and to revise the early drafts of the proposed new Anglican Covenant with an eye to the modification, expansion, and application of this classic and beloved text to the specific new historical moments and challenging contexts of the twenty-first century.

5

'From All Nations and Languages'
Reflections on Church, Catholicity and Culture[1]

CHARLOTTE METHUEN

'And how is it that we hear, each of us, in our own native language?' (Acts 2.8)

'After this I looked, and there was a great multitude that no one could count, from all nations and tribes, peoples and languages.' (Rev. 7.9)

'Tradition is not the worship of ashes, but the passing on of the fire.' (Gustav Mahler)

Vincent of Lerins famously offered a definition of Catholic: 'that which has been believed everywhere, always, by everyone'. Reflecting on the catholicity of the Old Catholic Church, the German Old Catholic Bishop Joachim Vobbe pointed out that, on the one hand, the church has never been 'catholic' in this sense.[2] The history of the Church makes it

---

1 This article appeared originally in German as '"Aus allen Nationen und Sprachen" – Überlegungen zu Kirche, Katholizität und Kultur', in Angela Berlis, Matthias Ring and Hubert Huppertz (eds), *Im Himmel Anker werfen: Festschrift für Bischof Joachim Vobbe zum 60. Geburtstag* (Bonn: Alt-Katholischen Bistumsverlag, 2007), pp. 265–75.

2 Joachim Vobbe, *Katholisch – ein altes Wort neu gesehen. Festvortrag 125 Jahre Altkatholisch Gemeinde Kempten im Allgäu* (Nördlingen: Bistum der Alt-Katholiken in Deutschland, 1999), pp. 8–9.

clear that there is no teaching and no dogma which has been believed everywhere, always, by everyone. The defining of the Canon of Scripture, the doctrines of the Trinity and Christ each resulted from a long and complex process, involving argument, conflict a dissent. Vobbe's remark offers a reminder that the Church has always had to mould itself to circumstance and context, and that this is a complex process. The Church must be alert to changes and developments if it is to continue to proclaim the Gospel in such a way as to be heard.

On the other hand, Vobbe recognized that the Church catholic has indeed existed always and everywhere, for 'in all churches, also in the churches of the Reformation, there have always been truly catholic people, whose faith has been founded on commitment to the Bible, to the shared confession and the richness of sacramental life.[3] The existence of the catholic Church in this sense shows the true meaning of the term 'catholic'. In its true sense, 'catholic' does not point to boundaries; it 'is not a means of drawing confessional boundaries, … not a label asserting ownership, but a word which expresses a relationship; in reality a truly dynamic, broad and open word'.[4] Derived from the Greek *'kath' holos'*, catholic means, not general, not even universal, but 'pertaining to the whole.' The Church is catholic precisely because – or precisely when – it seeks to take seriously its relationship to the whole.[5]

Vobbe's analysis points to the question which is currently exercising the Anglican Communion. In New Testament terms, how can the Church hold together the glorious experience of Pentecost, 'We hear, each of us, in our own native language' (Acts 2.8), with the vision of St John the

---

3   Vobbe, *Katholisch*, p. 9.
4   Vobbe, *Katholisch*, pp. 9–10.
5   Vobbe, *Katholisch*, p. 10.

Divine: 'After this I looked, and there was a great multitude that no one could count, from every nation, from all tribes and peoples and languages, standing before the throne and before the Lamb, robed in white, with palm branches in their hands' (Rev. 7.9)? That is, how can the particularity of the Church – the particular gift of being able to preach the Gospel in every context – at the same time become an expression of the Church's catholicity, its being so as to pertain to the whole?

This is in no way a new question. In his seminal work *The Gospel and the Catholic Church*,[6] Michael Ramsey insists that the historical church always is and will remain partial, and that it is necessary to distinguish between the imperfection of historical manifestations of the Church and the Church's catholicity: 'the essence of Catholicism all through the ages has consisted not in partial systems – such as Papal government or Greek theology – which have been both its servants and its dividers, but in the unbreakable life to which the sacraments, scriptures, creeds, and ministry have never ceased to bear witness'.[7] For Ramsey, this deeper sense of catholicity points to the true, God-given unity of the Church, for it shows that that unity already exists, 'not in what Christians say or think, but in what God is doing in the one race day by day. The outward recovery of unity comes not from improvised policies, but from faith in the treasure which is in the Church already.'[8] Recovery of the Church's unity 'is hindered whenever Catholicism is identified with something less than itself, and whenever the definition of it is based on what is really local, temporary, partial'.[9] The Church points 'beyond theology, beyond reunion-schemes, beyond philanthropies, to the death

---

6   A. Michael Ramsey, *The Gospel and the Catholic Church* (London: Longmans, 1936).

7   Ramsey, *Gospel and the Catholic Church*, p. 175.

8   Ramsey, *Gospel and the Catholic Church*, p. 175.

9   Ramsey, *Gospel and the Catholic Church*, p. 175.

of the Messiah. It leads the theologian, the church-statesman, the philanthropist and itself also to the Cross'.[10] The true catholicity of the Church – and with it the Church's unity, apostolicity and holiness – become visible in the truth of the death and resurrection of Christ, through the preaching and living out of that truth in discipleship, and in the recognition that *a church* which preaches and follows that truth is indeed *the Church*, the body of Christ. For Ramsey, the preaching of the Gospel defines the catholicity of the Church, for it is in that preaching that it is apparent that the nature of the Church is to be *kath' holos*.

Ramsey understands the partiality of the Church confessionally: no one confessional church can manifest the fullness of catholicity, whether it be Roman Catholic, Orthodox, Lutheran, Reformed, Old Catholic, Anglican or any other. The plurality of the Anglican Church is an important but partial hint of catholicity. For Ramsey, as also for Hans Küng, the fulfilled, perfect, ideal church does not – and cannot – exist in this world. The church in this world is the visible church, which exists within history and must take form in history.[11] Nevertheless, despite its imperfection and its historical contingency, the church as is really exists

> is sent into the world as sign, instrument and first-fruits of a reality which comes from beyond history, the Kingdom, or reign of God … . The Church is thus a *provisional embodiment* of God's final purpose for all human beings and for all creation. It is an *embodiment* because it is a body of actual men and women chosen by God to share through the Spirit in the life of Christ and so in his ministry in the world. It is *provisional* …

---

10   Ramsey, *Gospel and the Catholic Church*, p. 9.
11   Hans Küng, *Die Kirche* (Freiburg: Herder, 1967), pp. 14–15.

[because] only part of the human family has been brought into its life, and those who have been so brought are only partly conformed to God's purposes.[12]

The Church's provisionality is rooted in the fact that the Word of the Gospel is a living Word. Just as musicians make music from the notes printed on the page, the Church takes the printed words of Scripture and, with the help of theology and liturgy, proclaims the living Word of God for the here and now.[13] It is the responsibility of the Church to pass on the fire, and not to worship ashes, as Gustav Mahler once put it. For 'the freedom, to respond in fresh ways in the face of new challenges is what enables the Church to be faithful to the Tradition which it carries forward'.[14] This is true, not only chronologically, for different ages and eras, but also geographically and culturally. If the Word of God is to be always and everywhere the Living Word – that is, if the Church which proclaims that Word is to be catholic – then the Word must be interpreted and translated for here and now, which is to say, for the particular context. If the Church is to continue to preach the Word of God to a changing world, then the Church cannot always be the same.

Characteristic of the work of interpreters and translators is the realization that there is never a simple mapping from one language to another. Words spoken or statements made in one language sound different in another. In his Prologue to the

---

12 House of Bishops, *Apostolicity and Succession* (London: General Synod of the Church of England, 1994), §32.
13 Alfred Rauhaus, Sermon to the Meissen Commission, 11 September 2006.
14 The Anglican/Roman Catholic International Commission (ARCIC), *Mary. Grace and Hope in Christ. An Agreed Statement* (Harrisburg and London: Morehouse, 2005), §3.

Book of Jesus Sirach, the Greek translator points to this problem:

> You are invited therefore to read it with goodwill and attention, and to be indulgent in cases where, despite our diligent labour in translating, we may seem to have rendered some phrases imperfectly. For what was originally expressed in Hebrew does not have exactly the same sense when translated into another language. Not only this book, but even the Law itself, the Prophecies, and the rest of the books differ not a little when read in the original.[15]

Every language is shaped by and itself helps to shape a different way of thinking. Consequently the fundamental truths of the Gospel will be heard and understood differently in each different language. Translations of the Bible, the preaching of the Word: both are shaped by the particular language – and in their turn shape the way in which the proclamation is heard. In preaching, the Word of God is interpreted and translated not only confessionally but also culturally. The Church as the place where the Word of God is preached is thus shaped not only by its confessional but also by its cultural identity.

That every church would have its own cultural specificity was clear to nineteenth-century missionaries. Edward White Benson (1829–1896), Archbishop of Canterbury from 1882, wrote of the Anglican Mission to Japan that 'the great end of our planting a Church in Japan is that there may be a *Japanese* Church, not an English Church'.[16] The Methodist Mission to

---

15   Jesus Sirach, Translator's Prologue, cited according to the NRSV.
16   A. C. Benson, *The Life of Edward White Benson* (London: Macmillan, 1900), vol. ii, p. 467; cited according to Mark Chapman, 'The Politics of Episcopacy', in Ingolf Dalferth and Paul Oppenheim

Fiji showed the problems of interpretation or translation needed to make such mission successful, and the consequent problems of defining the unity of the Church:

> This is the real difficulty: not even to transplant one's dear mother Church to a climate where it will wither, but so to master her principles and to enter into foreign intelligences as to raise up Churches truly native. It requires large wisdom abroad and great forbearance at home to work out an ideal of the Catholic church, so various and yet one.[17]

To ignore cultural difference when founding a church would be condemn the mission to failure:

> to seek to build up a like Church, stone by stone as it were, spiritually, out of the utterly different characters, experiences, sentiments of another race, is to repeat without excuse the error of the great Boniface, in making not a Teutonic but an Italian Church in Germany. It is to contradict the wise axioms with which Gregory tried to save Augustine [of Canterbury] from the error.[18]

Although Benson's distinction between the Church founded by Boniface in Germany and that founded by Augustine in England probably says at least as much about the situation of

---

(eds), *Einheit bezeugen: Zehn Jahre nach der Meissen Erklärung / Witnessing to Unity: Ten Years after the Meissen Declaration* (Frankfurt a. M.: Lembeck, 2003), pp. 150–70, here p. 167 (italics in the original).

17 Benson, *The Life of Edward White Benson*, p. 466; cited in Chapman, 'The Politics of Episcopacy', p. 167.

18 Benson, *The Life of Edward White Benson*, p. 466; cited in Chapman, 'The Politics of Episcopacy', pp. 167–8.

the late nineteenth-century Church of England as about his historical acumen, his argument is worthy of attention: a mission which attempts to found a church which is entirely foreign to its cultural context cannot succeed; the Gospel must be spoken – preached – in such a way that it can be heard and understood.

The era of the Reformation was shaped by the notion of the national church, not only in Protestant, but also in Catholic countries.[19] This is expressed in the principle of *cuius regio eius religio*, which was adopted formally for the Holy Roman Empire 1555 as a foundational element of the Peace of Augsburg, but in practice shaped many parts of Europe. Ecclesiastical identity became an important aspect of the definition of political identity, and in almost all cases, this was an identity which was catholic in the sense of including all who lived in a given geographical area.[20] English ecclesiastics of the sixteenth and seventeenth centuries thus understood the Church of England to be the catholic Church in England.[21] In early-modern Europe, the distinctive cultural aspects of the Gospel were understood in national terms and were indeed used to foster the development of national identity.

The concept of national churches has persisted. It underlay Edward White Benson's considerations of the importance of culture, and it was important to the conception and

---

19 Thus the Spanish Catholic Church had characteristic differences to the French Catholic Church. For the history of the Church in Spain and in France during the sixteenth century, see for instance Diarmaid MacCulloch, *Reformation: Europe's House Divided 1490-1700* (London: Allen Lane, 2003), pp. 417–426, 474–484.

20 France was something of an exception to this in the recognition given to the Huguenots under the Peace of Nantes alongside the Roman Catholic Church.

21 See, for instance, John Jewel, *An Apology for the Church of England* (1562), in: John Ayre (ed.), *The Works of John Jewel* (Cambridge: Cambridge University Press, 1848), vol. i, pp. 100–102.

establishment of the Anglican Communion. From the first Lambeth Conference in 1867, the Anglican Communion was shaped by its concern that there should be only one Anglican Church in any one country.[22] At the 1908 Lambeth Conference the Bishops passed a resolution which defined this principle not only in terms of confession, but also with reference to ecclesiological and linguistic concerns:

> [The Bishops] earnestly deprecate the setting up of a new organised body in regions where a Church with apostolic ministry and Catholic doctrine offers religious privileges without the imposition of uncatholic terms of communion, *more especially in cases where no difference of language or nationality exists.*[23]

---

22 This concern is expressed in many of the Resolutions and Recommendations of successive Lambeth Conferences from 1867 (found at: www.lambethconference.org/resolutions/index.cfm). The 1867 Conference sought to resolve a threatened schism after the consecration of J. W. Colenso as Bishop of Natal in South Africa (Lambeth Conference 1867, Resolutions 6 and 7). For the 'Colenso Affair' see Owen Chadwick, *The Victorian Church* (London: A & C Black, second edition, 1972), vol. ii, pp. 90–7; on the 1867 Lambeth Conference see esp. p. 94. In 1878 the Lambeth Conference attempted to resolve the problem of 'overlapping' dioceses and jurisdictions, and to avoid competition between the Church of England and the Protestant Episcopal Church of the USA, for instance by clarifying the situation in Continental Europe: 'as a general rule, … two chapels shall not be established where one is sufficient for the members of both Churches, American and English' (Lambeth Conference 1878, Recommendation 12.2; Encyclical Letter 4.2).

23 Lambeth Conference 1908, Resolution 69 (italics added by the author). The continued existence of overlapping Anglican jurisdictions in continental Europe and the existence of both Church of England chaplaincies and parishes of the Episcopal Church (USA) in Rome, Geneva and Paris shows both that this Resolution

The Resolution was passed in protest against the activities of the English Old Catholic Bishop Arnold Harris Mathew;[24] its effect is to define the cultural shaping of the local church – and with it the particularity of every manifestation of Church – in terms of a complex interaction between language, nationality and confession.

The cultural, national and linguistic shape of particular churches cannot, however, simply be accepted uncritically. The history of the twentieth century has made this very clear. The rise of the so-called *völkische Theologie* in Germany[25] and the appalling use made of it under the Third Reich, in particular (but not only) by the German Christians is an example of the dangers of allowing the preaching of the Gospel to be entirely subordinated to cultural concerns. In Germany the Church became effectively the tool of the totalitarian regime;[26] a similar observation could be made of the Roman Catholic Church in Spain under Franco. The ideology of *völkische Theologie* with its assumptions that racial difference must manifest itself in ecclesiastical specificity has parallels in the ordering of churches along racial grounds –

---

    has not been rigorously enforced, but also the strongly felt need of many who live abroad to worship in their own language.

24 See Christoph Schuler, *The Mathew Affair. The failure to establish an Old Catholic Church in England in the context of Anglican Old Catholic relations between 1902 and 1925* (Amersfoort: Stichting Centraal Oud-Katholiek Boekhuis, 1997).

25 The term is virtually untranslatable, but might perhaps best be rendered 'racial theology'. It refers to the idea that each race – and in particular Germans and Jews – has its own characteristic expression of religion.

26 There are many discussions of the Church in the Third Reich. For the theological aspects of National Socialist ideology, see Richard Steigmann-Gall, *The Holy Reich: Nazi Conceptions of Christianity, 1919-1945* (Cambridge: Cambridge University Press, 2004).

whether national or in terms of skin colour – which was long widespread practice in many North American churches, particularly in the Southern States, and in South Africa. The 1930 Lambeth Conference deplored such developments:

> The Conference affirms its conviction that all communicants without distinction of race or colour should have access in any church to the Holy Table of the Lord, and that no one should be excluded from worship in any church on account of colour or race. Further, it urges that where, owing to diversity of language or custom, Christians of different races normally worship apart, special occasions should be sought for united services and corporate communion in order to witness to the unity of the Body of Christ.[27]

They were particularly concerned that such arrangements must never lead to structural or legal inequality, emphasising that 'Christian principles demand that equal justice be assured to every member of every community both from the government and in the courts of law.'[28] Further, the Bishops emphasized that the validity of orders or the acceptability of ministry must never be regarded as in any way understood to be related to skin colour or race:

> The Conference would remind all Christian people that the ministrations of the clergy should never be rejected on grounds of colour or race, and in this connection it would state its opinion that in the interests of true unity it is undesirable that in any given

---

27 Lambeth Conference 1930, Resolution 22.
28 Lambeth Conference 1930, Resolution 21.

area there should be two or more bishops of the same Communion exercising independent jurisdiction.[29]

For many parts of the British Empire of the 1930s – and thus for much of the Anglican Church – this was a strongly counter-cultural statement. The Lambeth 1930 Resolutions offer an important reminder that not every cultural development can be accepted by the Church. The Church must take account of culture and adapt to it, but at the same time must stand in tension to culture.

The Church exists, therefore, in a critical tension to the culture in which it is embedded. In the Gospel of John, Jesus says of those who follow him: 'They do not belong to the world, just as I do not belong to the world' (Jn 17.16). This description expresses the critical distance which the Church needs to take towards the world, and thus to the culture within which it exists, but at the same time it marks the need for awareness of the gifts and the challenges that God offers through the world. Christ's relationship to this world is not other-worldly, not world hating, but deeply rooted in human joy and pain, that is, in the reality of human experience. Christ's ministry is shaped by the needs and experiences of the people he encounters, through which he offers insight and meaning. Those who are excluded from society are often precisely those whom he explicitly addresses and calls into his discipleship. The Gospel speaks into their experience – into their culture, with their language – precisely in order to challenge them to bring their experiences into dialogue with the Gospel. Joris Vercammen, Old Catholic Archbishop of Utrecht, speaks of the calling 'to a living dialogue between

---

29   Lambeth Conference 1930, Resolution 22.

Christian faith and culture, to the benefit of both'.[30] This dialogue is, he believes, an essential aspect of the being and responsibility of the Church. The early church demonstrates how culture and faith are intertwined, and the Church needs to learn from that,

> looking for glimpses of the Holy Spirit in one another, but also criticizing degrading developments. In accusing the evil and praising the Lord for all good things that have come about, the church contributes to a spiritual process needed by societies in order to become more human.[31]

Helping societies become more human – to recognize all members of society as created *imago Dei* – is the calling of the Church. It is also an expression of the Church's catholicity, for to become more human is to recognize the full humanity of others, to engage with others and to become ever more deeply aware that one's own discipleship is shaped by the ways in which others seek to follow Christ.

The catholicity of the Church means that the fullness of the Gospel – and therefore of discipleship – can never be realized through one person's response to the call of Christ, or within the specificity of any one culture or language or confession. Rather the catholicity of the Church is manifested in the realization of the multiplicity of ways in which followers of Christ have responded to its call. Rowan Williams sees this realization – and with it the sense of standing in relationship with all other who have sought to follow Christ – as a

---

30 Joris Vercammen, 'Die Hoffnung unserer Berufung (Eph. 4,4). Vortrag beim 29. Internationalen Alt-Katholiken-Kongress in Freiburg, 9. August 2006', in *Ökumenische Rundschau* 55 (2006), pp. 553–63, here p. 555.

31 Vercammen, 'Die Hoffnung', p. 555.

definitive moment in grasping what it means to be the Church which is the Body of Christ:

> Who I am as a Christian is something which, in theological terms, I could only answer fully on the impossible supposition that I could see and grasp how all other Christian lives had shaped mine, and more specifically, shaped it towards the likeness of Christ. I don't and can't know the dimension of this; but if I have read St Paul in I Corinthians carefully, I should be at least be thinking of my identity as a believer in terms of a whole immeasurable exchange of gifts, known and unknown, by which particular Christian lives are built up, an exchange no less vital and important for being frequently an exchange between living and dead. ... I do not know, theologically speaking, where my *debts* begin and end. How my progress towards the specific and unique likeness of Christ that is my calling is assisted by any of other Christian life is always going to be obscure.[32]

That is, the Church's catholicity requires all believers to recognize that their own specificity – whether individual or communal – cannot be the defining moment of what it is to be the Church of Christ, whilst at the same time celebrating the fact that the fullness of what it is to follow Christ – and thus the way that each believer answers that call – is shaped by the very fact of all the others. No-one is or can be a follower of Christ in isolation. The Catholic Church is greater than the church's existence in any specific time or place.

---

32 Rowan Williams, *Why Study the Past? The Quest for the Historical Church* (London: DLT, 2005), p. 27 (italics in the original).

This recognition is both a gift and a challenge. It offers a reminder that unity – and with it community and communion – can never imply uniformity. The multiplicity of ways in which the Gospel is heard shapes and forms the unity and community of the Church. As ARCIC has recognized:

> this diversity of traditions is the practical manifestation of catholicity and confirms rather than contradicts the vigour of Tradition. As God has created diversity among humans, so the Church's fidelity and identity require not uniformity of expression and formulation at all levels in all situations, but rather catholic diversity within the unity of communion. This richness of traditions is a vital resource for a reconciled humanity.[33]

Indeed, the diversity and multiplicity encountered through the catholicity of the Church is the foundation of the Church's community and of its unity. That is:

> The Church's catholicity expresses the depth of the wisdom of the Creator. Human beings were created by God in his love with such diversity in order that they might participate in that love by sharing with one

---

33 ARCIC, *The Gift of Authority.* (Authority in the Church III) *An Agreed Statement by the Anglican/Roman Catholic International Commission* (Toronto: Anglican Bk. Centre; London: Catholic Truth society; New York: Church Publishing, 1999), §27. For an overview of the work of ARCIC with links to the various reports, see: http://www.prounione.urbe.it/diaint/arcic/e_arcic-info.html

another both what they have and what they are, thus enriching each other in their mutual communion.[34]

The catholicity of the Church exists in the mutual enrichment of all who honestly follow Christ.

This does not, however, mean that the whole to which the Church in its catholicity pertains – the '*kath' holos*' of the Church – is simply a matter of adding together the different parts. The fullness of the Church – its catholicity – means much more than that the various different personal, confessional, cultural receptions of the Gospel exist alongside one another. Catholicity is realized through a lived and living deep encounter between those varying apprehensions of the Gospel. This relationship is something like the encounter between two languages or cultures, which can offer a route to deeper meaning and fresh understandings of familiar ideas. For me, such an encounter came when I heard Matthew 13.44 read for the first time in German: 'The kingdom of heaven is like treasure hidden in a field, which someone found and hid; then in his joy he goes and sells all that he has and buys that field.' In English 'treasure' often has connotations of ownership and hoarding – the pirate's treasure, buried in the sand – and it can be difficult to hear this parable as teaching anything other than a focus on personal gain. In German, the 'treasure in the field' becomes 'der Schatz im Acker' – a direct translation, except that the word 'Schatz' has clear connotations not only of 'expensive', 'costly' but also of 'beloved'. 'Schatz' is also the German translation of 'darling'. Through hearing the parable in German, I understood for the first time that the kingdom of God is about an encounter with

---

34 ARCIC, *The Church as Communion. An Agreed Statement, August 28–September 6, 1990, Dublin, Ireland* (London: ACC and Catholic Truth Society, 1991), §35.

something that one loves so much that one is prepared to give up everything for its sake. The interaction between the languages opened up for me a deeper understanding of this parable and revealed to me a new aspect of the kingdom.

This is in many ways a trivial example, but it illustrates the way in which the encounter between different languages can open up different and deeper meanings and reveal unexpected connections. Such an encounter reveals also a deeper sense of translation: the deep encounter between two languages makes possible, not simply finding ways of saying (more or less) the same thing in different words, but understanding how the words of different languages, with their different associations, can inform and explain one another. The encounter with another language can show the limitations of one's native language: German has no single word for 'commitment', and does not distinguish between 'atonement' and 'reconciliation'; but it can expressively speak of God's salvific promise (*Verheißung*) and of the security found with God (*Verborgenheit*) in ways which are closed to English. An encounter with another language reveals the possibilities and limitations of one's native language, while at the same time opening up new ways of thinking about the world which would not be possible in one's language alone. Those bilingual children who grow up believing that they speak one language while everyone else can only speak half, have an important insight. The deeper meanings revealed through the encounter between languages point to the true character of what it means to be '*kath' holos*', and thus to catholicity.

A deep encounter between different languages assumes a willingness to learn the other language. This recognition can also be illuminating when considering the catholicity of the Church. Rowan Williams has spoken of the necessity of 'speaking the language of Anglicanism'. Leaving aside the vexed question of how such a language might be defined, the metaphorical association of confession with language offers a helpful approach to considering the different levels of meaning of the term 'Catholic'. For if it is possible to speak of a 'language of Anglicanism', and then it must also be possible to speak of a language of Old Catholicism, of Roman Catholicism, of Lutheranism, of Orthodoxy. None of these 'languages' would be easily defined, but each would say something about a shared identity. In this sense, the term 'Catholic' (further qualified as 'Old Catholic', 'Roman Catholic') is confessional and refers to a particular ecclesiastical identity. Within this one 'language' there can also be 'dialects', defined by the specificity of local expressions of those global communions.[35] Like any spoken language, a confessional language will not be everywhere identical. Nevertheless, the words of one English speaker will be (more or less) comprehensible to those of another.

Individual languages make up language groups. So too, in the language of confessions there are confessional families or wider ecumenical groupings. On this level the term 'Catholic' is also used, alongside 'Protestant' or 'Orthodox'. Those who are 'Catholic' in that they point to the importance of liturgy and sacrament, a focus on Church Order, an emphasis on Tradition, are using the term in this sense.

---

35 This is true not only of the global communions such as the Anglicans or Lutherans, but also of the Roman Catholic Church. The theologian Teresa Berger has commented on the many different expressions and understandings of Roman Catholicism which are gathered together in the Roman Catholic Church in Durham NC: 'In the face of such diversity, the interesting question naturally presents itself: what makes us all Catholic?' Teresa Berger, 'Über-Setzen. Eine theologisch-biographische Zwischenbilanz', in Katharina von Kellenbach and Susanne Scholz (eds), *Zwischen-Räume* (Münster: LIT, 2000), pp. 93–100, here p. 97.

Finally, the metaphor of confessional language points to the fact that human beings are not trapped within one language. Almost everyone would be able – although not everyone is necessarily willing – to learn another language and in that way to discover a fresh and different way of looking at the world. The human capability of learning another language is what makes new and enriching encounters between cultures and ways of thinking possible. This is a third sense of catholicity.

The metaphor of language shows the limitations of any definition of the true catholicity of the Church which places it in one of the first two categories. The catholicity of the Church cannot belong to one confession or group of confessions. To suppose that it does is like suggesting that only English is capable of describing the world. Some English-speakers might be tempted to believe this is so, but speakers of other languages would surely not agree. No language and no language group can claim to describe the world fully. This metaphor of confessional language points to the fact that the catholicity of the Church must lie deeper. If the Church is to be truly catholic, if it is really to be '*kath' holos*', to pertain to the whole, then it must strive always to translate and interpret between the different languages in which the Gospel is heard and spoken, allowing those encounters to reveal deeper meaning.

The catholicity of the Church lies in the ability of the people of God to engage in this process. To be catholic is not to speak a particular confessional language, to belong to a particular confessional grouping, but to partake of the God-given capability of learning to speak another (confessional) language than one's own, and through it to demonstrate an – also God-given – openness to deeper encounter and through it the recognition of the unity which is God's gift to the Church. The Church's catholicity calls every follower of Christ to take seriously their responsibility as translator, and interpreter of each other's words and understandings of the Gospel.

Christians are thus called to become builders of bridges, and it is surely no accident that this is the original meaning of *pontifex*. Bishops are called particularly to build bridges, to enable this process, to take responsibility for the internal ecumenism of enabling differing groups to learn to speak to one another. The catholicity of the Church – its *'kath' holos'* – enables and requires each member of the people of God to look beyond their particular expression of church, and to allow their own particular expression to deepen and be deepened by others. In that sense, every congregation, every diocese, every province, every confession is made in the image of the Church Catholic. And every congregation, every diocese, every province, every confession needs structures to enable encounters of catholicity to happen, and to ensure that such encounters really do take place.

6

The Anglican Covenant:
An African Perspective

VICTOR ATTA-BAFFOE

The Windsor Report advances the establishment of The Anglican Covenant, which will be entered into by the Churches of the Communion as they seek to walk together as Anglicans, and deepen their commitment to a visible communion within Anglicanism. This chapter comments on the Covenant from an African (especially Akan of Ghana) perspective. It argues that while the idea of the covenant is laudable for the common good of the Anglican Communion it must not be approached from a legal but rather from a missiological and pastoral point of view. It further points out that the effect of the covenant rests less on structures and instruments of the Communion and more on relationships across different peoples and cultures in service to the mission of God.

Setting the Context

The Lambeth Commission on Communion was called as a result of the decisions of the 74th General Convention of the Episcopal Church (USA) 'to appoint a pricst in a committcd same sex relationship as one of its Bishops and of the Diocese of New Westminster (Canada) to authorize service for use in connection with the same sex union'.[1] However, it is important to note that the Report makes clear the fact that the issues facing the Communion are broader and deeper than the actions which led to the calling of the Commission.[2]

The Windsor Report provides an opportunity for the Anglican Communion to consider a crucial and necessary approach to the way forward in order for it to grow and develop in a mature and faithful way. The process implies intentional, focused hard work among all the members of the Communion. The underlying concern of *The Windsor Report* focuses on ecclesiological questions and how that might help us to understand the nature and mission of the Anglican Communion. For all practical purposes, the report does not attempt to resolve conflicts or the crisis relating to sexuality and homosexuality in particular, which seem to pull the Communion apart.

No one denies the fact that the Anglican Communion is in crisis, and that there are more questions than answers. Underneath the Report are some major questions such as: What does it mean to be Anglican in a pluralistic world? What can we use to describe Anglicanism in the twenty-first century? How can Anglicans live together as a Communion in the face of the differences and diversity as a worldwide community of faith? These questions raise for the Communion both ecclesiological and missiological concerns, and for that matter, bring into sharp focus the crisis – Identity crisis – facing the Communion today.

One systemic indicator of the Anglican Communion is that it is extraordinarily diverse. For this reason, the fragility of its unity is exposed by wide differences over some issues, not least

---

1   *The Windsor Report* (London: The Anglican Communion Office, 2004), §1.
2   *TWR* §43.

of which is human sexuality. The tensions that have characterized the Communion over human sexuality have revealed the 'north-south' divide. Similarly, they are considered as a battle between 'truth' and 'falsehood', between 'the righteous' and 'sinners', between 'orthodoxy' and 'apostasy'. The challenge of these tensions is not helpful because it does not allow people to appreciate the deeper ecclesiological and missiological issues that underlie our unity-in-diversity.

Consequently people lay the blame for the tensions and disunity either on the arrogance and theological liberalism of some churches (that is, those of the Global North) or on the biblical fundamentalism of some churches (that is, those in the Global South). Against this background, we fail to see the beauty of Anglicanism and indeed Christianity. Any attempt to define and enforce some universal Anglican norm or ethos brings with it the risk of denying the necessity of diverse, contextual way of being Christian and doing mission. The beauty of Anglicanism is that there is no single way of being Anglican.

This idea that characterizes the spirit of Anglicanism in its life and practice is what one may consider as *progressive orthodoxy*.[3] The idea embraces the tension between the old and the new, between the universal nature and the particularity of the Christian gospel. *Progressive orthodoxy* is rooted in the faith inherited from the early Church, yet open to new concepts and insights in the light of contemporary understanding of the

---

3   The concept of what might be called 'progressive orthodoxy' is typified by Paul Avis's approach in his book, *Anglicanism and the Christian Church* (Edinburgh: T&T Clark, 1989; new edition, 2002). However, it should be said that the approach is fundamental to Anglican ecclesiology, and it is also evident in the works of most Anglican theologians. Particularly, this concept corresponds to Richard Hooker's ecclesiology.

reality within which the faith is preached and lived out in the diverse cultural contexts of a pluralistic society. The traditional self-understanding of Anglicanism is that it enhances local difference and also sees the diversity of the Anglican family as a source of enrichment.

The above observation lies at the heart of the Anglican Communion. It remains at this point to look at the covenant and Anglicanism, and to consider some cultural assumptions from an African (especially, Akan of Ghana) perspective, and to show how they might inform the understanding of global Anglicanism.

Covenant and Anglicanism

The Hebrew word *berith* has normally been translated 'covenant'. It is a solemn pledge that is taken or imposed and is accompanied by a rule. It is a mutual pledging, whereby each partner commits himself or herself to an agreed course of action. There are several mentions of covenant in the Bible. For example, in the priestly tradition of Genesis 9.1–17 there is the covenant between God and Noah after the flood. There are two accounts of a covenant with Abraham, a Yahwist tradition in Genesis 15.18 and a Priestly tradition in Genesis 17. In Exodus 19 and 20 we have the great covenant between Yahweh and the Israelites, which is renewed in Jeremiah 31.31ff. Then, of course, there is the new covenant sealed with the blood of Christ.

In the *berith* involving Noah after the flood, the rainbow is interpreted as a reminder that the human race shall endure, however transient the individual. One significant feature about the *berith* is the emphasis on community. The human race implied by the *berith* is a community and should live as a community. In connection with this idea is the second essential feature of the sanctity of human life. The life of each and every human is sacred and it is a condition for living in community. The biblical ideas captured in the *berith* correspond with the thinking of the Akan. In shaping a theology of humanity the twin ideas of community and sanctity of each and every life cannot be overlooked.

The Sinaitic *berith* constitutes yet again a people of God as a community. The terms of the *berith* deal with obligation to God[4] and obligations to fellow human beings.[5] The list of obligations to fellow human beings – honouring and respecting one's parents (and elders), not murdering, not committing adultery, not stealing, not bearing false witness, not coveting a neighbour's anything – are all things that make for a cohesive community and therefore, for the dignity of all who live in communion with each other. In other words, the Decalogue, for all practical purposes, is not some abstract mystical thoughts but is about the mechanisms and props for good community living and for human dignity, which, of course, are inseparable from one's obligations to God. The New Testament puts it as loving God and loving one's neighbour as oneself.[6] This is epitomized in the sharing of one bread and one cup at the Eucharistic table.

The ramifications of this obligation for our Christian life and community living implies that whoever cannot practically show love to other persons *de facto* denies their dignity and by the same token cannot be themselves truly human. The *berith* theme therefore speaks of a number of issues in human life: sanctity of life, living in community with justice and integrity and of human dignity. With this emphasis on sense of community we will look at Akan thought and philosophy and

---

4   Exod. 20.1–11.
5   Exod. 20.12–17.
6   Mk 12.28–31; Rom. 13.8–10.

147

how that might contribute to global Anglicanism as it struggles to realize the Church as the people of God.

Covenant and Akan Epistemology

One aspect of the Akan world-view, which needs our attention here, is the *sensus communis*, which is based on the epistemology of *cognatus sum, ergo sum*. In contrast to René Descartes dictum: *cogito ergo sum* – 'I think, therefore I exist' – the claim that holds for *homo Akanus* is *cognatus sum, ergo sum* – 'I exist because I belong to a family'.[7] A sense of community as opposed to a very individualistic culture is of the essence of being human.

The *sensus communis* shows a deep-seated desire to ensure that everybody is related to all in various ways. The sense of community and communality of traditional society has held its own in spite of increasing individualism and also increased mobility. The sense of community in Akan thought and philosophy is by no means a limiting factor upon the individual's self-expression.

The Akan sense of community does not sacrifice individual aspiration. Each person aspires to develop a full personality and identity as an individual; nevertheless such a development cannot be divorced from his or her role as a member of the family. Akan, like most Ghanaian peoples, believe that it is only through being rooted in a corporate organism of solidarity, co-existence and co-responsibility that the existence of each individual and that of the community can be

---

7   See John S. Pobee, *Toward an African Theology* (Nashville: Abingdon, 1979), p. 49. The concept of *sensus communis*, Pobee believes, is an element the African (Akan) shares with the biblical faith, and is therefore a basis upon which a dialogue may be begun (pp. 44ff).

guaranteed and realized. This is not to say that the individual is an object of manipulation in the hands of the community. On the contrary, he or she is a unique subject. The individual stands paramount when it concerns his or her survival, growth and personhood. When the individual values are at stake the community recedes into the background and gives the full weight and support to the individual. But there are moments in which community values stand in the forefront, and the individual must recede into the background and give support to them. Just as they do not accept that the community value should degenerate into totalitarianism or 'community-absolutism', where individual liberty and personal freedom are suppressed or unduly curtailed in the community, they do not tolerate that individuality should develop or degenerate into callous individualism.

Laudable as the epistemology may be, it is ultimately defective in so far as the unit is the blood group. It is good so far as it goes in that the idea requires sharing among members of the extended family. But of course, those who are beyond the blood group are also people with dignity, and created in the image of God. They also need to be beneficiaries. If a modern society or Communion, which is poly-ethnic and multicultural, is to cohere, kin-groups cannot be a key factor in the *sensus communis*.

To that extent, I submit that the traditional Akan *sensus communis* is a *praeparatio evangelica* for what Christian theology offers. Nevertheless, I argue also, that in the context of Anglicanism communion needs to be developed on the basis of the traditional Akan insights of what human community consists in, namely, belonging to a community and being cared for by the community in return for someone also making a contribution one way or another. These and other social values in Akan traditional society offer profound insights upon which Christians can build. The concept of epistemology of the Akan is at once individual as well as communitarian. It is comprehensive, multifaceted and holistic. It is with this set of ideas or concepts that Anglicanism must engage.

There is one important question we ought to ask: what is the essence of the Covenant? Simply put, the Covenant is about the mechanism that we need to hold the Communion together. In that case, it is about relationship, and therefore, an occasion for re-visiting the principles that Anglicanism has stood for.[8] Communion within Anglicanism is relational. As expressed in *The Virginia Report*, it is a gift from God that is lived through the power of the Holy Spirit.[9] This communion is lived out by Anglicans in different socio-political cultures to serve and advance God's mission of reconciliation and transformation. This task is reinforced by *The Windsor Report*:

> This communion is primarily a relationship with God, who is himself a communion of Father, Son and Holy Spirit, and it binds every member of Christ into the whole body. Our communion enables us, in mutual interdependence, to engage in our primary task, which is to take forward God's mission to his needy and much-loved world.[10]

---

8 For example, the 'Mutual Responsibility and Interdependence in the Body of Christ' (MRI). This concept emerged from the Toronto meeting of the Pan-Anglican Congress in 1963. See Stephen Fielding Bayne, *Mutual Responsibility and Interdependence in the Body of Christ* (New York: Seabury, 1963).

9 Inter-Anglican Theological and Doctrinal Commission, *The Virginia Report: the Report of the Inter-Anglican Theological and Doctrinal Commission* (included in James M. Rosenthal and Nicola Currie (eds), *Being Anglican in the Third Millennium* (Harrisburg PA: Morehouse, 1997), pp. 211–81, chap. 2.

10 *TWR* §§45, 46. See also Appendix Two, Article 6.

In the light of that, the Communion must begin to listen to the insights of the different regions.

There is room for listening and to allow the process to sink into the hearts of people. Thus the idea of covenant must not be approached from the legal but rather from the missiological and pastoral point of view. The Communion as a theological community must ensure that the key determinant in the drawing up of the Covenant is the emphasis on the responsibility of all for all and of each for each, rather than simply stressing 'my right' and 'your right'. The undergirding principle of the Covenant must be the 'ethic of responsibility' rather than the 'ethic of individual rights'. *The Windsor Report* specifically states this in the preliminary draft of the Anglican Covenant:

> Each member Church belongs to each other in mutual reciprocity and forbearance in the Body of Christ. Communion does not require acceptance by every Church of all theological opinion, sacramental devotion, or liturgical practice that is characteristic of the other. Every member Church has the intention to listen, speak, act and strive to obey the gospel. Every Church has the same concern for a conscientious interpretation of scripture in the light of tradition and reason, to be in dialogue with those who dissent form that interpretation, and to heal divisions.[11]

Instead of seeing the Covenant as an attempt to expel people with whom we disagree from the Communion, it must be an opportunity to build up strong tics and rclationships bctwccn members of the Communion and of all with God. The conversation must be guided by passion, trust and Christian

---

11   *TWR* App. 2, Art. 4.

charity. Talking across borders will simply not solve the problem, neither will it enhance the mission of the Church. Listening to someone with passion, trust and Christian charity requires that one must be willing to engage with the other and to allow oneself to be affected by the situation of the other. Writing the covenant is not enough. We must keep talking and listen to what the Spirit is saying to the churches.

The so-called younger churches are old enough to be considered as partners in their own right, and therefore must be listened to seriously. The shift of the centre of gravity of the Communion from the Global North to the Global South cannot be overlooked. However, as someone from the Global South, I dare to say that this shift must not only be measured in terms of numbers – of churches, people and even bishops, but also by the depth of faith and commitment to the Gospel values. There are several examples of abuse of children and women, as well as other problems, including HIV/AIDS, nepotism, tribalism, inter-ethnic and religious violence, and ethnocentrism. These are equally important missiological challenges for the Communion as human sexuality. Covenant in mission will therefore enhance the participation of common mission, and also promote the richness of diversity as a catalyst for enrichment in the Communion, and not as an impoverishing factor that can generate only conflicts and divisiveness.

Covenant and Communion in Spirit

Much has been said and written on the concept of *koinonia* as a central focus of communion, partnership, fellowship and other values that give support to mutuality and cooperation in Anglicanism.[12] The concept of *koinonia* is pivotal for expressing

---

12   See for example, *The Virginia Report*, chap. 2.

the character of the ethos that should exist among church members.[13] As far as the New Testament is concerned, it is a major task of the Christian Church. Alongside the theology of *koinonia* are such concepts as *oikonomia* (stewardship), *oikodome* (building up, edification), and *katallage* (reconciliation). These concepts are definitive characteristics of the Church in action. Thus, even if it would be possible to place greater emphasis on *koinonia* as the foundation of our life together in the Church, the people – the Church, the body of Christ – must faithfully live out the meaning of this foundation in terms of their commitment to stewardship, edification and reconciliation. For all practical purposes, this must truly bring meaning to the embodiment of *koinonia* itself.

The creation of Adam in the Bible is not just the story of an individual but it is about humanity. Thus creation and humanity go together. And humanity is about *koinonia*. The creation story continues with the story of the fall. The original community was disoriented and disturbed through sin. The idea of sin as it is described in the story implies that it is idolatry in the sense of replacing God with, for example, wealth or power. But I also want to stress that sin is also a refusal to be brotherly or sisterly, as the story of Cain and Abel demonstrates. The story of Cain and Abel is the paradigm into which the denials of human dignity, whether by poverty, unjust economic order, dictatorship or injustice fit.

In a lecture the Akan scholar, G. P. Hagan has commented: 'Unity emerges when we discover and put together the different chips, which make up the solution of the national

---

13 Suffice it to say that the working out of the practical, theological and liturgical implications of this theme continues to undergird much of the ecclesial and ecumenical advances.

(communal) jig-saw puzzle.'[14] *Koinonia* is created neither by numbers nor by proximity; it is created by the sense that one needs the other person to define oneself and the meaning of one's existence, and that our lives do influence others for good or for ill. By means of this sense our acts and deeds enrich or impoverish others, and vice versa. In the New Testament, the new humanity through the last Adam – Christ – is described in the context of a community that has been forgiven, has had its burden of guilt removed and therefore, has a new sense of their worth as human beings. This biblical insight of communion is continuous with the Akan sense of communion, though not identical. For the traditional Akan sense of communion and community is very much kin-group based. To that extent, it could be said, it is a rather narrow sense of community. What Christianity has to offer is a community that goes beyond the kin-group to include all manner of people. *Koinonia* – communion – in this sense, as it is expressed in Baptism and the Eucharist, is a sharing of life, material and non-material resources for the benefit of all. It is being able to communicate love and thus live in the community of faith, the Church.

The vision of *koinonia* is a gracious gift and a divine mandate from God. It calls the Church into a life of mutual participation (relationships) in each other's lives and circumstances. *The Windsor Report* affirms this participation in God's mission as bases to understanding communion: 'This grace-given and grace-full mission from God, and communion with God, determine our relationship with one another. Communion with God and one another in Christ is thus both

---

14 G. P. Hagan, 'Human Rights and the Democratic Process', in *Symposium on the Concept and Practice of Human Rights in Ghana* (Ghana Academy of Arts and Sciences, 21st Anniversary Celebration, November, 1980).

a gift and a divine expectation.'[15] It is the effectual working out of this theological vision of *koinonia* that can in some way help the Anglican Communion as a whole to overcome at least some of the conceptual, attitudinal, intercultural and organizational difficulties that have afflicted the Communion over the years. We can certainly attempt to bring new understandings to bear on the central meaning and message of the Gospel to which we are committed as the fundamental source of faith. Efforts over time have provided the Communion with innumerable lessons for living together in Communion, and they have helped to shape and re-shape our sense of Communion and identity, not so much in terms of what we have, or who we are, but more so in terms of who we can become, by God's grace.

The innumerable personal encounters which Anglicans have with one another, and which reinforce their sense of common faith and authentic spirituality, more than attest to the fact that the measure of true fellowship or communion within the Anglican Communion really consists of the power of the Spirit at work between those who acknowledge and demonstrate their need for one another, rather than simply coveting one another's treasures. It exists at the level of having nothing, while yet possessing all things. It thrives on the mutual interdependence and acceptance of one another's presence and not on the mutual acquaintance with one another's power. It flourishes at the level of sharing in one another's pain and possibility, and has nothing to do with one another's prominence or popularity. Dispersed authenticity within global Anglicanism then, must come alive in the myriad ways by which we help one another to live towards our common need of God, and our joint search for God in all the convulsive and

---

15   *TWR* §5.

surprising ways in which we can walk together, talk together, discern together, discover together and celebrate together.

7

Towards an Anglican Covenant: A Roman Catholic Perspective

PAUL MCPARTLAN

'We know that in everything God works for good with those who love him'. (Rom. 8.28)

The Anglican Communion is currently facing grave issues of structural unity at the same time as it seeks to clarify its teaching on important sacramental and moral issues. The two sets of issues (structural and doctrinal) are intimately related, in that the Church as a pilgrim people is bound to encounter new challenges and unforeseen questions on its journey in history, and therefore must have an adequate mechanism for coping with them and finding acceptable solutions which, far from placing the community under stress, actually consolidate its unity. Serious issues will inevitably test the structures, and it would surely be an unlikely luxury to be able to work out the structures prior to addressing any major problems. It is far more likely that problems will precipitate work to establish adequate structures, and St Paul assures us in the above passage that that process and its end result can be blessed if the work is done in the love that is the gift of God.

This has been the pattern of the life of the Church ever since the earliest centuries, and there are almost countless historical precedents that might be looked to for guidance and help in the present situation. The fourth century was a particularly turbulent period of doctrinal crisis and structural upheaval. Henry Chadwick writes:

> It was the misfortune of the fourth-century Church that it became engrossed in a theological controversy at the same time as it was working out its institutional organisation. The doctrinal disagreements quickly became inextricably associated with matters of order, discipline and authority. Above all, they became bound up with the gradually growing tension between the Greek East and the Latin West.[1]

As indicated above, I would suggest that what was indeed obviously a 'misfortune' from one point of view, can also be seen as perhaps providential from another. By its very name, the Anglican Communion proclaims its awareness that God's gift to us is a participation in the communion life of the Trinity. Now, as well as being a communion in space, as it were, uniting Christians across the world today, the Church is also a communion in time, and tradition is the fellowship of Christians through the ages, by means of which those who face problems today can be helped in charity by those who have gone before us marked with the sign of faith. From the

---

1 Henry Chadwick, *The Early Church* (Harmondsworth: Penguin, revised edition, 1993), p. 133. Part of this quotation was used in the Report submitted to the Lambeth Commission by an ad hoc sub-commission of the International Anglican-Roman Catholic Commission for Unity and Mission (IARCCUM): 'Ecclesiological Reflections on the Current Situation in the Anglican Communion in the Light of ARCIC' (8 June 2004), n. 5 (in a section of the report devoted to 'The Church's Life in the Fourth Century'). I shall refer to this text as 'IARCCUM Report'. It was published in the Pontifical Council for Promoting Christian Unity, *Information Service*, n. 119 (2005/III), pp. 102–15.

many important legacies of the fourth century, I would like to consider one particular canon from that century that is playing a prominent role in ecclesial and ecumenical reflection today, and that, I would like to suggest, can be helpful in the process of preparing an Anglican Covenant.

The quotation from Henry Chadwick valuably highlights the fact that already in the fourth century, long before the famous events of 1054, there were tensions between the Greek East and the Latin West precisely with regard to the structure of the Church and the manner of resolving doctrinal and disciplinary disputes. One of the most hopeful ecclesial events of recent times has been the resumption of formal dialogue between the Roman Catholic Church and the Orthodox Church, aimed at the restoration of full communion. The first meeting of the largely reconstituted Joint International Commission for Theological Dialogue between the Roman Catholic Church and the Orthodox Church was held at Belgrade in September 2006, and was swiftly followed by Pope Benedict's highly successful visit to Turkey, and in particular to the Ecumenical Patriarchate of Constantinople, in November 2006. The dialogue has reached the crucial stage of considering the interrelated topics of authority, conciliarity and primacy in the Church.

It would surely be helpful for the Anglican Communion, which has been in fruitful dialogue for decades with both of these churches individually,[2] to bear the Roman Catholic-

---

2   With regard to dialogue with the Roman Catholic Church, see the many agreed statements of the Anglican-Roman Catholic International Commission (ARCIC) and the recent agreed statement of IARCCUM, *Growing Together in Unity and Mission* (2007). With regard to dialogue with the Orthodox Church, see the Moscow Agreed Statement (1976), the Dublin Agreed Statement (1984), and the recently published Cyprus Agreed Statement, *The Church of the Triune God* (2007).

Orthodox (RC-O) dialogue in mind as it (the Anglican Communion) moves towards an internal Covenant that will adequately accommodate considerations of authority, conciliarity and primacy in the polity of the Communion. Two particular reasons stand out. First, the RC-O dialogue is naturally seeking to draw on the period of the undivided Church in its reflections. That period belongs to the heritage of us all, including Anglicans, and offers principles that have stood the test of time subsequently. Principles that come to prominence in the dialogue because of their relevance for Roman Catholics and Orthodox today, may well be relevant also for the Anglican Covenant. Second, the more there are common threads running through the decisions that Catholics, Orthodox and Anglicans make both individually and together in this privileged ecumenical time, the more we shall implicitly be weaving the fabric of ever greater unity.

It is not at all surprising that the Anglican Communion, which because of a variety of factors has seen a rapidly increasing number of provinces in the past century, should be grappling with the crucial issue of how to coordinate the life of such a diverse and burgeoning family of Christians. The Communion has progressively provided itself with four instruments of unity, namely the Archbishop of Canterbury, the Lambeth Conference, the Anglican Consultative Council, and the Primates' Meeting. A clear recognition that the Christian Church needs both primacy and conciliarity in its structures of authority is evident in the list of these instruments, yet these instruments as presently constituted have not proved sufficient to deal with the present crisis in the Communion. Precisely because these instruments already embody recognition of the crucial principles of primacy and conciliarity, the way forward lies not in abandoning them for other instruments, but in developing them to serve more adequately.

The lack of an explicit body of canon law specifically pertaining to the Communion as such has also been keenly felt. *The Windsor Report* of 2004 strongly supported moves towards furnishing the Communion at least with a body of canonical principles (*TWR* §114), and such a *corpus* would indeed seem to have a vital role to play as an additional instrument of unity. However, *The Windsor Report*'s most prominent proposals focus upon the Archbishop of Canterbury himself and aim at strengthening his primatial role (*TWR* §§105–12). Given the origins of the Church of England and hence of the Anglican Communion, it is natural that there should be an instinctive caution with regard to a primacy pertaining to the Communion as a whole, yet the need for a stronger focal primacy has become plain.

Mutatis mutandis, there is great caution regarding universal primacy among the Orthodox Churches, yet a constructive dialogue on primacy, including universal primacy, has begun among Orthodox and Roman Catholics. The latter, of course, are known for a universal primacy so strong that it has risked eclipsing conciliarity. After the definitions of papal primacy and infallibility at Vatican I (1869–70), it gradually became widely presumed that the era of councils was now over. Pope John XXIII caused a major stir by the very fact of summoning another council. At its heart, appropriately, was a definition of the collegiality and collegial responsibility of the bishops:

> The order of bishops is the successor of the college of the apostles in their role as teachers and pastors, and in it the apostolic college is perpetuated. Together with their head, the Supreme Pontiff, and never apart

from him, they have supreme and full authority over the universal Church.[3]

The most significant thing about Vatican II (1962–65) was that it actually happened. The conciliar experience 'reopened the chapter in the Church's book of conciliar life'.[4]

The third agreed statement of the international Roman Catholic-Orthodox dialogue stated that it was in the perspective of 'communion among local churches that the question could be addressed of primacy in the Church in general and in particular, the primacy of the bishop of Rome'. Moreover, it invoked a fourth-century canon, namely Apostolic Canon 34, to indicate a way forward: 'according to canon 34 of the Apostolic Canons, belonging to the canonical tradition of our churches, the first among the bishops only takes a decision in agreement with the other bishops and the latter take no important decision without the agreement of the first'.[5] This canon would likewise, I presume, be counted as belonging to the canonical tradition of the Anglican Communion. It may be of great benefit to the Communion at this time, as it is certainly offering assistance in the context of RC-O dialogue. It is also perhaps worth mentioning that, although the Orthodox do not favour the concept of Canon

---

3   Vatican II, Dogmatic Constitution on the Church, *Lumen Gentium*, §22.

4   Yves Congar, 'A Last Look at the Council', in Alberic Stacpoole (ed.), *Vatican II by those who were there* (London: Geoffrey Chapman, 1986), pp. 337–58, here p. 341.

5   'The Sacrament of Order in the Sacramental Structure of the Church with Particular Reference to the Importance of Apostolic Succession for the Sanctification and Unity of the People of God' (1988), in John Borelli and John H. Erickson (eds), *The Quest for Unity: Orthodox and Catholics in Dialogue* (Crestwood/Washington DC: St Vladimir's Seminary Press/United States Catholic Conference, 1996), §§55, 53, respectively (here p. 142).

Law, an awareness of the *Canons* is crucial to Orthodox ecclesial life. Canons do not have to be viewed purely as matters of *law*.

The value of Apostolic Canon 34 for RC-O dialogue has been strongly advocated by Metropolitan John Zizioulas of Pergamon, the Orthodox Co-President of the international RC-O dialogue (the Catholic Co-President being Cardinal Walter Kasper). Recently, Metropolitan John went so far as to state: 'This canon can be the golden rule of the theology of primacy.'[6] The full version of the canon is as follows:

> The bishops of every nation (region = *ethnos*) ought to know who is the first one (*protos*) among them, and to esteem him as their head, and not to do any great thing without his consent; but every one to manage the affairs that belong to his own diocese and the territory subject to it. But let him (i.e. the first one) not do anything without the consent of all the other (bishops); for it is by this means that there will be unanimity, and God will be glorified through Christ in the Holy Spirit.[7]

Zizioulas regards the Trinitarian doxology at the end of the canon as highly significant. It indicates that this manner of relating between what he calls the 'one' and the 'many' has its prototype in God, and is the pattern that the earthly Church must necessarily adopt if it is truly participating in the life of God. In other words, communion is not a vague or formless

---

6   Ioannis Zizioulas, 'Recent Discussions on Primacy in Orthodox Ecclesiology', in Cardinal Walter Kasper (ed.), *The Petrine Ministry* (Mahwah, NJ: Newman Press, 2006), pp. 231–46, here at p. 243.

7   John D. Zizioulas, *Being as Communion* (London: Darton, Longman & Todd, 1985), pp. 135–36, n. 24. There was a reference to this canon in IARCCUM Report, §8.

reality. It has a definite *shape*, namely that of the one and the many. This fact is of great importance for the shaping and structure of a Trinitarian, communional Church. In the Trinity, the Father is the *one*, the central, anchoring Person, of whom the Son is begotten and from whom the Spirit proceeds. There are no Son and Spirit without the Father, but equally there is no Father without the Son and the Spirit. There is full reciprocity between the one and the many. This pattern then applies to Christology, to the Eucharist, and to the Church, which regularly *receives communion* in the celebration of the Eucharist.[8]

Zizioulas continues: 'the one-and-the-many idea which runs through the entire doctrine of the Church leads directly to the ministry of primacy'. Primacy is the reflection of the 'one' in the structure and life of the Church. He adds: 'It [the one-and-the-many idea] also indicates the conditions which are necessary for primacy to be ecclesiologically justifiable and sound.'[9] It is important to note that, although Canon 34 originally applies at the *regional* level, Zizioulas sees in it a principle that must logically apply at *all* levels in the Church, *local* (the bishop in his local church), *regional* (e.g. the primate or patriarch among the bishops of an area), and *universal* (the universal primate among the primates or patriarchs). 'A

---

8   See also Metropolitan John (Zizioulas) of Pergamon, 'Primacy in the Church: An Orthodox Approach', in James F. Puglisi (ed.), *Petrine Ministry and the Unity of the Church* (Collegeville: Liturgical Press, 1999), pp. 115–25, here pp. 118–19. Also, *Being as Communion*, pp. 135–37. On Zizioulas, see my book, *The Eucharist Makes the Church: Henri de Lubac and John Zizioulas in Dialogue* (1993; new edition, Fairfax, VA: Eastern Christian Publications, 2006), esp. pp. 203–11; also my article, 'The Local Church and the Universal Church: Zizioulas and the Ratzinger-Kasper Debate', in *International Journal for the study of the Christian Church* 4 (2004), pp. 21–33.

9   Metropolitan John, 'Primacy in the Church', p. 121.

universal *primus* exercising his primacy in such a way is not only "useful" to the Church but an ecclesiological necessity in a unified Church.'[10]

A Russian Orthodox theologian, Nicolas Lossky, indicates that Zizioulas speaks 'for all of us [Orthodox]' with regard to the ecclesiology of communion, and he also highlights the earlier use of Canon 34 to refer to primacy at *all* levels in the Church by Father Alexander Schmemann.[11] Two nuanced quotations from Schmemann may serve to indicate the kind of (universal) primacy he would see as required by the Church:

[P]rimacy in the Church is not 'supreme power', this notion being incompatible with the nature of the Church as Body of Christ. But neither is primacy a mere 'chairmanship' if one understands this term in its modern, parliamentary and democratic connotations.[12]

---

10 Metropolitan John, 'Primacy in the Church', p. 125. See also Metropolitan John of Pergamon, 'The Church as Communion: A Presentation on the World Conference Theme', in Thomas F. Best and Gunther Gassmann (eds), *On the way to Fuller Koinonia* (Faith and Order Paper no.166) (Geneva: WCC, 1994), pp. 103–11, esp. p. 108. See also pp. 106–7, where Zizioulas says that 'the careful balance between the "one" and the "many" in the structure of the community is to be discovered behind all canonical provisions in the early church'.

11 Nicolas Lossky, 'Conciliarity-Primacy in a Russian Orthodox Perspective', in Puglisi (ed.), *Petrine Ministry*, pp. 127–35, here at p. 131.

12 Alexander Schmemann, 'The Idea Of Primacy In Orthodox Ecclesiology', in John Meyendorff (ed.), *The Primacy of Peter* (first edition, 1963, new edition, Crestwood: St Vladimir's Seminary Press, 1992), pp.145-71, here p. 164; see p. 161 for Apostolic Canon 34.

Primacy *is* power, but as power it is not different from the power of a bishop in each church. It is not a *higher power* but indeed the same power, only expressed, manifested, realized by one. The primate *can* speak for all because the Church is one and because the power he exercises is the power of each bishop and of all bishops. And he *must* speak for all because this very unity and agreement require, in order to be efficient, a special organ of expression, a mouth, a voice. Primacy is thus a necessity because therein is the expression and manifestation of the unity of the churches as being the unity of *the* Church. And it is important to remember that the primate, as we know him from our canonical tradition, is always the bishop of a local church and not a 'bishop at large', and that primacy belongs to him precisely because of his status in his own church.[13]

I would respectfully propose that Schmemann's description of primacy (which it is interesting to compare with the definition of papal primacy by Vatican I) may be useful to the Anglican Communion at the present time on several counts. First, it offers a frank, confident and unapologetic case for a real primacy, not just at the regional level, but also at the universal level. Schmemann's words resonate at many points with the needs, desires and priorities of the Anglican Communion at this time. They also, I suggest, prompt a query about something stated in *The Windsor Report*. 'Like the other Instruments of Unity, ... the Primates' Meeting has refused to acknowledge anything more than a consultative and advisory authority' (*TWR* §104). By its phrasing, this statement

---

13 Schmemann, 'The Idea Of Primacy', p. 165; cf. Metropolitan John, 'The Church as Communion', p. 108.

presumably includes reference to the authority of the Archbishop of Canterbury also. Schmemann's primate has more than just a 'consultative and advisory authority', and his primacy certainly goes beyond what is often presumed to apply in Orthodoxy, namely a 'primacy of honour' (the phrase which is applied in *TWR*, App. Two, Art. 24, to the position of the Archbishop of Canterbury).[14]

Second, Schmemann emphasizes, as does Zizioulas even more strongly, that primacy and synodality (or conciliarity) go *together* and are not alternatives. There is no synod without a primate, and no primate without a synod; that is the point of Canon 34.[15] *The Windsor Report* is rather tentative in its promotion of the idea of a real primacy for the Archbishop of Canterbury in the Communion as a whole, as if there is a weakness humanly and perhaps even theologically in the fact that, unlike the other instruments of unity, 'he alone is an individual, and not conciliar in nature'. He will thus need to be 'supported by appropriate mechanisms to ensure that he does not feel exposed and left to act entirely alone' (*TWR* §§111–12). What seems to be absent here is the fundamental perception of the ontological interdependence of the one and the many that Schmemann and Zizioulas take for granted. Their primate *is* 'conciliar in nature'.

Third, Schmemann, and Zizioulas after him, are highly critical of the distortion of Orthodox ecclesiology by religious nationalism and autocephaly. 'All these "autocephalies" are absolutely equal among themselves, and this equality excludes any universal centre or primacy.' The result, they say, is a Church 'naturalised' and 'reduced', conformed to the world

---

14 Cf. Zizioulas, 'Recent Discussions', p. 253: 'There seems, in fact, not to exist, even in the Orthodox Church, "a simple primacy of honour".'

and not to Christ.[16] This criticism mirrors the concern that *The Windsor Report* expresses regarding an excessive provincial autonomy which tends towards independence and resists the 'mutual interdependence' that ought to characterize a communion life rooted in God (e.g. *TWR* §§46, 49, 51, 66, 74, 76). Schmemann and Zizioulas indicate that universal primacy, rightly understood, is a proper and ancient institution to counter such a distortion.

Before moving on, it is important to highlight the obvious point that the Archbishop of Canterbury is not the universal primate that both Schmemann and Zizioulas have in mind in their writings on this subject! The universal primate they are considering is the Bishop of Rome. Both Anglicans and Roman Catholics have likewise agreed that '[t]he only see which makes any claim to universal primacy and which has exercised and still exercises such *episcope* is the see of Rome',[17] and that 'a universal primacy will be needed in a reunited Church and should appropriately be the primacy of the bishop of Rome'.[18] I do not for one moment wish to call into question these affirmations of ARCIC; rather the contrary. My application here of the thought of Schmemann and Zizioulas regarding universal primacy to the position of the Archbishop of Canterbury is by analogy. The Archbishop's position is one that falls somewhere in between the original regional level of Canon 34 (the level of the provinces with their primates) and the universal level to which Schmemann and Zizioulas extend the principle of the canon, with the universal primacy of Rome in view. It is precisely the *principle* of the canon that I

---

15   Cf. Schmemann, 'The Idea of Primacy', pp. 160–1; also Zizioulas, 'Recent Discussions', pp. 237, 243.

16   Schmemann, 'The Idea of Primacy', pp. 166–7; see also Zizioulas, 'Recent Discussions', p. 241.

17   ARCIC, Agreed Statement, *Authority in the Church I* (1976), §23.

18   ARCIC, Agreed Statement, *Authority in the Church II* (1981), §9.

am applying to the Archbishop's role, with the idea that, if Orthodox, Catholics and Anglicans all allow their structures to be shaped by the same principle (of the one and the many), then there will be an increasing 'family resemblance' between them, and it ought eventually to be easier to align and integrate those structures in one overall visible communion.

The idea of the 'interdependence' of churches in the Anglican Communion is of huge importance, and there is benefit in unpacking it both theologically and practically. Appendix Two of *The Windsor Report* ('Proposal for the Anglican Covenant') helpfully relates interdependence to the mystery of the Body of Christ and speaks of 'mutual reciprocity' between member churches (Art. 4). It then goes deeper still, and explores the dynamics of life in communion by saying that each church 'is constituted in, exists in and receives fullness of life in its relations to the other member churches' (Art. 7.2); each church is 'completed in, through and by its relations with other member churches' (Art. 8.1). The mystery being evoked in these descriptions of relationship is nothing less than the mystery of the Trinity itself, in which the communion life of the Body of Christ is ultimately rooted. The Appendix correctly applies to the member churches of the Communion the pattern of relations that exists between the divine Persons.

We may go further, and aptly speak of a *perichoresis* or 'mutual interiority' between the churches, and indeed between each member church and the Communion as a whole. What this ultimately means is that the bonds of communion that unite the member churches with one another and with the Archbishop of Canterbury as primate of the Communion are not *external* bonds, added to the autonomous lives of the respective churches *from outside*, but rather *internal* bonds that go to, and spring from, the heart of each autonomous church

169

itself, and form part of its own internal integrity.[19] These bonds form part of the very *constitution* and self-definition of each member church.

Two particular consequences may immediately be identified. First, the constitutions and canons of the member churches ought to reflect the fact that Communion membership is part of their self-definition, and should not give the impression that those churches are fully constituted prior to or aside from communion with the other churches and with the primate of the Communion. In other words, member churches should not be defined purely in themselves, for example, by their adherence to preaching the word, celebrating the sacraments, professing the creed, being in apostolic succession and committed to mission, etc., and then just 'happen', as it were, also to be members of the Communion. That would reduce the Communion simply to a society. In short, the Covenant needs to be *internalized* by each member church, and taken into its heart.

Second, *The Windsor Report* states that the instruments of unity exercise no jurisdiction *over* the autonomous member churches (*TWR* Art. 24). However, it must be clarified that that does not mean they have no authority with regard to member churches. This is a delicate but vital point. The idea of 'jurisdiction over' corresponds to the idea that bonds of communion (with other churches and likewise with the instruments of unity, including the primate of the Communion) are *external* to member churches. Problematically, our Western minds immediately think of the

---

19 See also Congregation for the Doctrine of the Faith (CDF), *Letter to the Bishops of the Catholic Church on Some Aspects of the Church Considered as Communion* (1992), §13, where, from a Catholic standpoint, the CDF states: 'The ministry of the successor of Peter ... is a necessary expression of that fundamental *mutual interiority* between universal Church and particular Church.'

word 'over' as the sequel to that of 'authority'. All authority is presumed to be authority *over*, and not to be serious unless it is *juridical*. Thus, if 'jurisdiction over' member churches is eschewed by the instruments of unity (as arguably it should be),[20] the danger is that those instruments are not regarded as having any *real* authority. It is therefore extremely important that learning about what might be called *authority-in-communion* (i.e. as pertaining to the instruments of unity) accompanies the process of learning about 'autonomy-in-communion', the concept that *The Windsor Report* wishes to promote (e.g. *TWR* §76, cf. §§40, 80, 82, 84). Authority-in-communion is the authority that an instrument has *within* the Communion precisely because of the internal dynamics of the life of communion; if anything it is *weightier* than mere 'jurisdiction over'. Appreciation of that fact needs to be nurtured.

The above reflections resonate in many ways with the valuable reflections contained in the consultation paper of the Joint Standing Committee, *Towards an Anglican Covenant* (hereafter, *TAC*),[21] and in the Inter-Anglican Theological and Doctrinal Commission text, *Responding to a Proposal of a Covenant* (hereafter, *IATDC*). Both texts look to what a growing Communion realistically needs in terms of structures to manage the conflicts and even crises that will inevitably arise on its journey as a pilgrim people (*TAC* §§10–11; *IATDC*, 3.1, 4.1, 4.5). Both texts see the Covenant as part of an organic development of the Communion as it seeks now to articulate, heal, strengthen and develop the very 'bonds of affection' that

---

20 Cf Schmemann, 'The Idea of Primacy', pp. 165–8; Zizioulas, 'Primacy in the Church', p. 124.
21 Joint Standing Committee, *Towards an Anglican Covenant: A Consultation Paper on the Covenant Proposal of the Windsor Report*, March 2006.

already unite it (*TAC* §§1, 6–7; *IATDC* 1.11, 6.1). *TAC* emphasizes the *educational* value of a Covenant (§§9, 17).

I would add the following specific comments:

(i) *Towards an Anglican Covenant* asks whether the Covenant might be short, like the Bonn Agreement (1931), which led to full communion between Old Catholics and the Anglican Communion, or the Lambeth-Chicago Quadrilateral of 1888 (*TAC* §17). I would remark that the three clauses of the Bonn Agreement, as stated,[22] fall short of what is required here, and that the recent crisis itself shows the inadequacy of the Quadrilateral as a covenantal formula. The Covenant must essentially include a mechanism for dealing with problems, a strong and satisfactory account of the *process* that will be followed. Appendix Two of *The Windsor Report* (Arts 23–27, but see my reservations above about Art. 24) seems to tackle this aspect well.

(ii) The somewhat delicate issue of the status and authority of the Lambeth Conference is indicated in both texts (*TAC* §17; *IATDC* 4.4). Whether the Lambeth Conference can and should continue to be simply an 'informal gathering of bishops' (*IATDC* 4.4) is a moot point. *The Windsor Report*, App. Two, Art. 24, says something stronger, namely that the Lambeth Conference expresses 'episcopal collegiality worldwide' and that it gathers for 'common counsel,

---

22 'Each Communion recognizes the catholicity and independence of the other and maintains its own. Each Communion agrees to admit members of the other Communion to participate in the Sacraments. Intercommunion does not require from either Communion the acceptance of all doctrinal opinion, sacramental devotion, or liturgical practice characteristic of the other but implies that each believes the other to hold all the essentials of the Christian faith.' (*TAC*, p. 4)

consultation and encouragement and to provide direction to the whole Communion'. Episcopal collegiality was understood by Vatican II to entail leadership of the Church,[23] and the history of the early Church shows the vital role of discernment and leadership played both by regional councils (cf. provincial synods) and by ecumenical councils. Obviously, the Lambeth Conference is not an 'ecumenical council'. Nevertheless, it is an extremely significant gathering of, in principle, all the bishops of the Anglican Communion, with their primates and the focal primate, the Archbishop of Canterbury. It was natural in the early Church for bishops to gather to resolve together issues of major importance, and for them to make binding decisions in council. Does the status of the Lambeth Conference itself now need clarification and perhaps enhancement?

(iii) Neither *TAC* nor *IATDC* particularly highlights the specific value of the Primates' Meeting as an instrument of unity, but, ecclesiologically speaking, the recent development of this instrument would seem to be an extremely positive move, very much in accord with the principle of Apostolic Canon 34. It might be worthwhile to bear that principle in mind as the relationship of the primates to the Archbishop of Canterbury is further articulated.

(iv) I would prefer the image of 'concentric circles' to that of 'two tiers' used by *TAC* to describe what might prove to be different degrees of commitment to an eventual Covenant (*TAC* §§32–3). Visually, the first image permits the Archbishop of Canterbury to be at the centre of the structure of communion, which is entirely appropriate.

---

23 See above, *Lumen Gentium*, §22.

In conclusion, I would emphasize my desire to advocate the use of common principles by Catholics, Orthodox and Anglicans at this important time of ecclesiological discussion and decision in various contexts, drawn from the common tradition that we are privileged to share. In so doing, by the grace of God, may we prepare the way for the eventual restoration of full communion between us all.

8

The Methodist Idea of Covenant

KENNETH WILSON

Methodism and the Idea of Covenant

'Covenant' is a term that refers to a voluntarily contracted relationship between two or more parties; it has early secular usage with regard to marriage and commercial agreements. But for the Jewish and Christian traditions it functions specially to characterize the relationship between God and humankind. I was taught that it always described the relationship of a superior to an inferior and implied some sort of condescension on the part of superior party. While there is of course truth in this point of view when considering the covenant of God with God's creation, one will only understand the illuminating perspective of the covenant relationship of God and humankind in the Christian tradition, if it is filled out more sensitively. The Wesleys, John and Charles, with their Arminian convictions understood this very well.

God's relationship with the creation is a covenant relation in the sense that it is of grace not a matter of obligation. Indeed it is an expression of God's Trinitarian nature of self-giving love, faithfulness and everlasting loving-kindness: the covenant, established through the Word 'says and does' how God is for the creation, not what God becomes out of pity for the world. It exists because God out of God's own desiring *wanted* to create a world with which God would be in eternal relationship. Humankind could not have forced it upon or required it of God. Nevertheless the worth that God attributes to the world and humankind by this commitment is such as to suggest that it could share qualities of divinity such as holiness.

Moreover, God's covenant is with the whole of creation. It is not confined to humankind, most especially not to a particular chosen portion of it foreordained to be saved. This, John Wesley believed is revealed in the Person of Jesus Christ. His life and teaching bear witness to the total inclusiveness of God's loving desire for the world to know him. For not even a sparrow falls without the knowledge of God, the Father of All. Nothing and no one is excluded. Wesley follows St John in affirming creation through the Word. Christ, the Word Incarnate, his teaching, death, resurrection and ascension are all aspects of the one thing that matters for the world's salvation, God's gracious presence in Christ, and in the power of the Holy Spirit.

Many things flow from this. No ecclesial structure can frustrate the will of God to bring the world to perfection. Hence, all may be saved.

> Come, sinners, to the gospel feast,
> Let every soul be Jesu's guest;
>> You need not one be left behind,
>> For God has bidden all mankind.[1]

Furthermore, all people without exception may know themselves forgiven, loved by God and therefore capable of

---

1   Charles Wesley in *Hymns and Psalms* (London, Methodist Publishing House, 1983), no. 460 (hereafter *HP*). This hymn was included in *A Collection of Hymns for the use of the People called Methodists* published by John Wesley in 1780. See Franz Hildebrandt and Oliver Beckerlegge (eds), *The Works of John Wesley* (Oxford: Clarendon Press, 1980), vol. vii, no. 2, p. 81.

perfection. The latter is a much misunderstood doctrine but it is at the heart of Wesley's theology. How could he deny it? Since a proper understanding of God means that God has committed himself in creation to bringing the world to God, it must be really possible for faithful Christians to know God and know themselves to be members of God's kingdom.

Of course it follows also that in a covenant relationship there are commitments and freedoms on both sides. The gracious freedom that is of the essence of God in God's self, also characterizes the world to which God has committed God's self. So just as the covenant established by God with his world is voluntarily chosen by God, so also ratification and acceptance of the covenant on the part of the believer depends upon the believer's free choice. Moreover, it demands not simply believing the faith in the sense of accepting the truth about God, Father, Son and Holy Spirit, but obedience to the vision in the sense that it is necessary to practise the faith in the virtues of the moral life. God's covenant with creation is eternal because it depends upon the nature of God and not the condition of the world. At the same time, enjoyment of the fruits of the covenant for humankind is not unconditional. It is a matter of free choice for each person. Moreover, the state of perfection which can be enjoyed, is not permanent – Wesley himself came to believe in his later years that it could be lost. Back-sliders beware!

The trouble for John Wesley was that the world did not see God in the same generous and gracious light as he did. Too frequently, God is thought to be beyond and outside human experience, standing in judgement over the world of humankind. Such awareness of God encourages fear and anxiety, not love and a desire to participate in God's life. It was the mission and passion of John Wesley to affirm in his life and work that nothing could be further from the truth. God was involved with his world, from its beginning to its end, in every dimension and for all people. His preaching to the miners at Kingswood and those whom he met on his onerous journeying on horseback through the length and breadth of England underlined Wesley's conviction that all were God's people, with souls to be saved, and all had opportunity to know it for themselves. Wesley's evangelism and the subsequent Methodist movement which he began, was the consequence of his clear recognition of God's covenant presence with his world and the freedom, peace and justice which was opened up when one had faith in such a God. Wesley set about spreading scriptural holiness through the whole of God's world which he regarded as his parish.

None of this was contrary to what Wesley understood to be his vocation as an ordained minister in the Church of England. In the tradition in which he stood, certainly since the Reformation, faith required both sound doctrine and good works. Thus, for example, *Faith and Good Works,* which Wesley produced in 1738, is a digest of five homilies prepared by Cranmer for former Catholic priests unused to preaching but now called upon to do so.[2] It went into nineteen editions during Wesley's lifetime and was a staple of Wesleyan theology.

Since Wesley saw no doctrinal conflict with his *alma mater* his natural impulse was to ensure that Methodist worship did not coincide with the worship of the parish church. However, he was only too aware of how the world and its temptations could seduce even the most ardent believer from the true faith. He therefore encouraged Methodists to meet in band and class meeting, to care for one another, share their concerns, intercede for the world, and build one another up. On such occasions too they sang hymns.

---

2   Albert C. Outler (ed.), *John Wesley* (New York, Oxford University Press, 1964), pp. 123–33.

All this was made clear as early as 1752 in *Predestination Calmly Considered*, a substantial piece of theological polemic in which Wesley exposed what he called the heresy of 'unconditional election'. God's covenant, through the Mediation of Christ is for all.[3]

> LX. ... 'To whom are the promises made, the promises of life and immortality?' The answer is, 'To Abraham and his seed'; that is, to those who 'walk in the steps of the faith of their father Abraham' [cf. Rom. 4.12]. To those who believe, as believers, are the Gospel promises made. To these hath the faithful God engaged that he will do what he hath spoken.

> LXI. This covenant of God I understand. But I have heard of another which I understand not. I have heard 'that God the Father made a covenant with his Son, before the world began, wherein the Son agreed to suffer such and such things, and the Father to give him such and such souls for a recompense; that in consequence of this, those souls *must* be saved, and those only, so that all others *must* be damned.' I beseech you where is this written? In what part of Scripture is this covenant to be found?

> LXII. The grand covenant which we allow to be mentioned therein is a covenant between God and man, established at the hands of a Mediator, 'who tasted death for every man' [Heb. 2.9], and thereby purchased it for all the children of men.

---

3   Outler, *John Wesley*, pp. 427–72.

The conditionality of this covenant is made clear, Wesley goes on to say, when after the Israelites had worshipped the golden calf, God renewed the covenant in the giving of the Law. We too have a new covenant that promises forgiveness of sins through the death of Christ in whose resurrection we can share. The Methodist understanding of covenant bears witness to a faithful and just God, who will fulfil the promise of eternal life to all who truly seek God through walking with Jesus Christ.

> Captain of Israel's host, and Guide
>   Of all who seek the land above,
> Beneath thy shadow we abide,
>   The cloud of thy protecting love;
> Our strength, thy grace; our rule, thy word;
> Our end, the glory of the Lord.

> By thine unerring Spirit led,
>   We shall not in the desert stray;
> We shall not full direction need,
>   Nor miss our providential way;
> As far from danger as from fear,
> While love, almighty love, is near.[4]

The Covenant and the Church

Wesley, it seems, never felt it necessary to rethink his view of the Church or the sacraments that he formed before the beginning of the Methodist societies. All the evidence is that he regarded Methodists as relying on the Church of England for sacramental practice and ecclesiological understanding. He was, he believed, an 'extraordinary minister' called to supply

---

4   Charles Wesley, *HP*, no. 62.

the deficiencies of practice which he found at the time in the ministry of the Established Church; it was not his vocation to subvert it and certainly not to replace it. In so far as he thought about it at all, he regarded Methodism as an evangelical order within the Church catholic, a view in which he was influenced both by the Puritan tradition and by his admiration for the Jesuits.

So where does the Church fit into Wesley's understanding of God and God's covenant with the world? In particular what about Methodism itself? The Church was called into being by Christ, the Word of God, in whose life, death, resurrection and ascension there was confirmed the eternity of God's covenant with the whole creation. Wesley would simply have been unable to take seriously the contemporary despair of many about the future of the Church.

> See the gospel church secure,
>   And founded on a rock;
> All her promises are sure;
>   Her bulwarks who can shock?
> Count her every precious shrine;
>   Tell to after-ages tell:
> Fortified by power divine,
>   The church can never fail.[5]

Wesley was forced to think about this matter later in his life most especially when 'ordaining' preachers for America in 1784 and later for England. He wrote a sermon *Of the Church* with a text from Ephesians:

> I beseech you that ye walk worthy of the vocation wherewith ye are called, with all lowliness and

---

5   *HP*, no. 438, v. 3.

meekness, with longsuffering, forbearing one another in love; endeavouring to keep the unity of the Spirit in the bond of peace. There is one body, and one Spirit, even as ye are called in one hope of your calling; one Lord, one faith, one baptism, one Lord and Father of all, who is above all, and through all, and in you all.[6]

In effect the sermon is a reflection on Wesley's own slightly abbreviated version of Article XIX of the Thirty-Nine Articles of Religion: 'The visible Church of Christ is a congregation of faithful men, in which the pure Word of God is preached, and the sacraments be duly administered.'[7]

Wesley judges that by the Church of Christ what was intended was a reference to the universal Church, rather than any one of the churches known to the New Testament world, or indeed any particular church as he knew the world of faith in the eighteenth century. Certainly this would be consistent with his sermon on the *Catholic Spirit* where his conviction is that what counts for the Christian is a shared faith in and love for God and one's fellow human beings, rather than doctrinal statements or worship practice.[8] Indeed while preaching the pure Word of God is an essential feature, as is the administration of the sacraments, he is loathe on his own judgement to exclude from the Church even those congregations where there may be some question about the truth of their doctrine or their celebration of the sacraments. This is because human beings must leave judgement to God, who with covenanting loving kindness may be trusted to be merciful. In addition, of course, Christians must 'walk worthy

---

6   Eph. 4.1-6. The sermon is printed in Outler, *Wesley*, pp. 308–17.
7   Outler, *Wesley*, p. 312.
8   John Wesley, *Forty-Four Sermons: Sermons on Several Occasions* (London: Epworth Press, 1944), pp. 442–56.

Kenneth Wilson

of the vocation wherewith we are called'. Belief is literally valueless unless expressed in behaviour that celebrates the community of faith _and_ the covenant of God with all creation.

The sacraments are Baptism and The Lord's Supper, both of which are of the _esse_ not simply the _bene esse_ of the Church. Wesley's thinking on baptism is based upon a publication of his father, Samuel Wesley in 1703. In 1756 John Wesley produced an abridged version of it, thus confirming his acceptance of his father's traditional Anglican position. Baptism is 'the initiatory sacrament which enters us into covenant with God'.[9]

> By baptism we enter into covenant with God, into that 'everlasting covenant' which 'he hath commanded for ever': that new covenant which he promised to make with the spiritual Israel, even to 'give them a new heart and a new spirit, to sprinkle clean water upon them' (of which the baptismal is only a figure) 'and to remember their sins and iniquities no more' – in a word, 'to be their God,' as he promised to Abraham in the evangelical covenant which he made with him and all his spiritual offspring.[10]

Perhaps more surprising, though it should not be so, is his insistence on the duty of constant communion. In his sermon on _The Means of Grace_, Wesley underlines the importance of outward material signs if our human body is to know and recognize the fact of God's presence with us. He writes:

> By 'means of grace,' I understand outward signs, words, or actions, ordained of God, and appointed for

9   Outler, _Wesley_, p. 319.
10 Outler, _Wesley_, p. 322.

183

this end, to be ordinary channels whereby he might convey to men, preventing, justifying or sanctifying grace.[11]

Both John and Charles Wesley were clear that while they may have difficulty with specific interpretations of the doctrine of transubstantiation, they were fully convinced of 'the real presence'.

> Jesus, we thus obey
>> Thy last and kindest word;
> Here, in thine own appointed way,
>> We come to meet thee, Lord.

> His presence makes the feast;
>> And now our spirits feel
> The glory not to be expressed,
>> The joy unspeakable.

> He bids us drink and eat
>> Imperishable food;
> He gives his flesh to be our meat,
>> And bids us drink his blood.

> Whate'er the Almighty can
>> To pardoned sinners give,
> The fullness of our God made man
>> We here with Christ receive.[12]

Wesley's teaching on the theology of Holy Communion is hardly original; indeed it owes much to Daniel Brevint.[13] He

---

11   *Forty-four Sermons*, Sermon XII, p. 136.
12   Charles Wesley, *HP*, no. 614, vv. 1, 3, 5, 6.

used an abbreviated version of his work as a preface to the 1745 publication of *Hymns on the Lord's Supper*. In a sermon called *On Attending the Church Service*, Wesley urges constant communion and deals with objections that might be raised to such encouragement. He states that Our Lord commands it, it brings benefit of assurance of sins forgiven, it is something for which one should prepare solemnly. Those who think they are not worthy, that it would be presumptuous to afford oneself of its benefits too regularly, that such frequency will lead to contempt for the sacrament through over familiarity, are simply ignorant of the fact that its spiritual vitality depends upon God not upon them. The covenant that God has with his creation and with his people is eternal, their commitment to celebrating this fact and sharing in the benefits must be analogically constant to be real.

The Covenant Service

The importance for Methodism of God's covenant with the creation and with the Church is apparent from the centrality given to the one unique contribution Methodists have made to the liturgical life of the Church catholic, the annual Covenant Service. It appears from Wesley's *Journal*, that the first institution of this service was in 1755,[14] but it grew rapidly and was a feature of the Conference in 1778, when Wesley reports, 'We solemnly renewed our covenant with God. It was a time never to be forgotten. God poured down upon the assembly the spirit of grace and supplication.' It has been a feature of Methodist worship ever since. The Wesleyan Conference revised it twice in the nineteenth century and the Methodist

---

13 *The Christian Sacrament and Sacrifice* (1673) (third edition, Oxford, 1749).

14 See John Wesley, *Journal* (entries for 6 and 11 August, 1755).

Church which emerged after the Deed of Union in 1932, included it in *The Book of Offices* of 1936. It was further revised in 1975 for *The Methodist Service Book,* and again in 1999 for *The Methodist Worship Book.*

On the many and increasing ecumenical occasions where it has been used, it has surprised and delighted by its formality, solemnity, grace and aura of serious delight and celebration. The God of Our Fathers, who has covenanted God's self to the well-being of his world in creating, and is now committed to its perfection through the redeeming life and work of Jesus Christ, invites all who have faith in God through Christ, to join him and share his self-giving love for the world.

The service itself moves from praise for the Trinity, to attending to scripture, confession and declaration of forgiveness, to the remarkably demanding words of the covenant itself, via prayers of intercession, to the sharing of the Body and Blood of Christ in the celebration of the Lord's Supper. The introduction to the most recent version of the service puts it like this:

> The emphasis of the whole service is on God's readiness to enfold us in generous love, not dependent on our deserving. Our response, also in love, springs with penitent joy from thankful recognition of God's grace. The covenant is not just a one-to-one transaction between individual and God, but the act of the whole faith community. The prayers of intercession which follow emphasize our unity with all humanity. The service proceeds to the Lord's Supper, for which a special form has been provided to emphasize the continuity between word, response and sacrament. The service is meant to lead us, by a path both similar to and differing from that of normal

Sunday worship, to that commitment which all worship seeks both to inspire and to strengthen.[15]

The congregation then sings the hymn which Charles Wesley wrote specially for the occasion:

> Come, let us use the grace divine,
>   And all, with one accord,
> In a perpetual cov'nant join
>   Ourselves to Christ the Lord:
>
> Give up ourselves, through Jesu's power,
>   His name to glorify;
> And promise, in this sacred hour,
>   For God to live and die.[16]

The presiding minister then declares the faith framework in which the people make the following public declaration. If one takes them seriously – and how can anyone say them insincerely?   the words are absolutely thrilling in their implication for all the world's life given the presence of God's commitment:

---

15 *The Methodist Worship Book* (Peterborough: The Methodist Publishing House, 1999), pp. 281–2. The service itself is found on pp. 282–96.

16 'A Collection of Hymns for the Use of the People called Methodists' in *The Works of John Wesley*, vol vii, no. 518, pp. 710–11. The editors note: 'This hymn's association with the annual Covenant Service goes back to Wesley's own practice.' See also John Wesley *Journal* (entry for 12 July 1778), and *HP*, no. 649, vv. 1, 2.

187

I am no longer my own but yours.
Put me to what you will,
    rank me with whom you will;
    put me to doing,
    put me to suffering:
let me be employed for you
    or laid aside for you;
let me be full,
    let me be empty,
let me have all things,
    let me have nothing;
I freely and wholeheartedly yield all things
    to your pleasure and disposal.

And now, glorious and blessed God,
Father, Son and Holy Spirit,
    you are mine and I am yours.
So be it.
And the covenant now made on earth,
    let it be ratified in heaven. Amen.

No words could make plainer the seriousness with which Methodists take the length and depth and breadth of God's covenant commitment to the creation and to all people of faith.

The Covenant People

The most recent statement of the Methodist Conference on ecclesiology draws attention to the Church as 'The Covenant People' and builds its interpretation of the role of the Church in the world, around this image.[17] The focus is on God, Father, Son and Holy Spirit, in whom the Church lives and works and has its being. It summons the community to pilgrimage, confident in the journeying mercies that God provides in the gospel of Jesus Christ, and in the promise of salvation and eternal life through him. Some words are worth quoting:

> At the heart of this Gospel is the revelation that God, as Father, Son and Holy Spirit, embraces the world, each member of the human race, and every living creature, with a love which not only creates, but re-creates and heals in the face of humankind's tragic, self-centred fragmentation. This is God's 'mission' to the world: God does not exist in isolation or detachment from creation, but with the passionate care of a father or mother engages with it, inviting humankind to find its lasting centre and home in the divine love. This love is the ultimate, inescapable centre and framework of all things. For this reason the Bible bears witness to the 'Kingdom' of God, for God, in spite of the dark abuses of human history, suffering and even death, 'reigns'. The climax to the Biblical testimony to both the mission and kingdom of God is the crucifixion and resurrection of Jesus – God's ultimate act of solidarity with and sacrifice for the world, and God's definite victory over evil. Out of this Gospel, the Church gladly acknowledges its vocation to celebrate the love of God in its worship, to share his life in its fellowship, and to be the agent of his generosity and compassion in a needy world.[18]

---

17 *Called to Love and Praise: A Methodist Conference Statement on the Church* (Peterborough: The Methodist Publishing House, 1999).

18 *Called to Love and Praise*, 5.2, p. 54.

And, profoundly, Methodism itself takes seriously the terms of its commitment to the covenant when later in the same statement it accepts the implications of its own words:

> I am no longer my own but yours. ... let me be employed for you or paid aside for you, ... Let me have all things, let me have nothing: I freely and wholeheartedly yield all things to your pleasure and disposal.

The Conference statement goes on:

> The Church for which this Statement is primarily written, the British Methodist Church, may cease to exist as a separate Church entity during the twenty-first century, if continuing progress towards Christian unity is made. If that happens, it is to be hoped that Methodism will be able to contribute some of the riches of its own distinctive history to any future Church.

The Anglican-Methodist Covenant, fraught with difficulties as it is, is an earnest of such commitment. And if, God willing, there is further movement towards organic unity of the two traditions, one might hope that the Methodist understanding of God's covenanting relationship with his world may be confirmed within the united body, and the Covenant service itself be a mark of its public faith. The future hope is captured by this hymn of Charles Wesley:

> Forth in thy name, O Lord, I go
>   My daily labour to pursue,
> Thee, only thee, resolved to know
>   In all I think, or speak, or do.

The task thy wisdom has assigned
   O let me cheerfully fulfil,
In all my works thy presence find,
   And prove thy good and perfect will.

Thee may I set at my right hand,
   Whose eyes my inmost substance see,
And labour one at thy command,
   And offer all my works to thee.

Give me to bear thy easy yoke,
   And every moment watch and pray,
And still to things eternal look
   And hasten to the glorious day;

For thee delightfully employ
   Whate'er thy bounteous grace has given,
And run my course with even joy,
   And closely walk with thee to heaven.[19]

---

19 'A Collection of Hymns for the Use of the People called Methodists', in *The Works of John Wesley*, vii, no. 315, p. 470. *HP*, no. 381. See also *Hymns Ancient and Modern New Standard* (Norwich: Hymns Ancient and Modern Limited, 1983), no. 239.

9

Covenant in the Bible and Today

JOHN BARTON

In *Towards an Anglican Covenant* we read:

> While the word 'covenant' is used to translate and
> describe the nature of a wide variety of relationships in
> the Old Testament, its most frequent use is when a
> divine initiative is met with a human response. The
> covenant holds out a promise by God which is fulfilled
> in the faithful response of his people. When there is a
> failure in faithfulness, a re-commitment is made ...
> The covenant relationship with God generates a
> covenantal relationship between his people.[1]

This bears very little resemblance to the understanding of
covenant language by most biblical scholars. It confuses the
idea of a covenant between God and his people with the
relationship of people to each other within the people of God,
which is never described as a covenant in the Old Testament.
That God makes promises to his people, which they 'covenant'
to respond to by obedience, *and that this entails that they are then
in a covenant relationship with each other*, is a purely Christian
idea and has no real parallels in the Old Testament.

---

1   Joint Standing Committee, *Towards an Anglican Covenant: A
    Consultation Paper on the Covenant Proposal of the Windsor Report*
    (London: Anglican Communion Office, 2006), p. 3.

If we examine the use of covenant language in the Bible on its own terms, we find in fact a very complicated picture. To sum up a great deal of modern scholarly work on this topic, best surveyed by Ernest Nicholson in his book *God and his People: Covenant and Theology in the Old Testament*,[2] 'covenant' is a way of describing a relationship of mutual commitment between two parties, which probably derives from its original secular meaning, 'treaty' – seen in the covenant made between David and Jonathan or between nations such as Israel and Aram in the historical books of the Bible. The relationship between God and people that is summed up in the word covenant may stress one of three things.

First, it may emphasize the element of divine initiative in entering into the relationship and being committed to it, so that the covenant is primarily envisaged as a kind of gift from God to the nation. This is perhaps the original meaning of the covenant with David, described in 2 Samuel 7, where God's making a covenant with David and his descendants means that he promises to be on the side of David's dynasty, to protect them from their enemies, and to ensure that the succession never fails. God's covenant with Abraham is also primarily promissory: it is an act of divine grace and mercy, choosing Abraham and promising to be with him and his descendants. This corresponds to the secular use of the term covenant in modern English in the context of charitable giving, where making out a covenant in favour of a particular charity means obliging oneself to pay them so much at regular intervals, and does not imply any particular action on their part. A mutual relationship is implied, but all the stress falls upon one partner giving freely to the other. The covenant with Noah after the Flood is of this kind: God simply promises that he will never

---

2   Ernest Nicholson, *God and his People: Covenant and Theology in the Old Testament* (Oxford: Oxford University Press, 1986).

again destroy this earth. This is his solemn *covenant*, or promise.

Secondly, and conversely, the stress may fall on the obligations imposed on the covenant partner by the person making the covenant. This is how the term is often used in the Psalms, and sometimes in parts of the Pentateuch, where God's *covenant* is more or less synonymous with God's law. The secular analogy would be a covenant in the deeds of a house, which oblige the owner on whom it is imposed to do or not to do certain things, such as observing rights of way. Here the emphasis is on what one of the partners is expected by the other to do. Psalm 25 says: 'All the paths of the Lord are mercy and faithfulness to such as keep his covenant and his decrees'. *Covenant* and *decrees* are here used as synonyms for the obligations which God lays upon his people. The general consensus among Old Testament scholars is that this use of the term appears in later parts of the Hebrew Bible, those written some time after the exile in the sixth century. Covenant became, at least for a time, more or less equivalent to law or Torah: the obedience which God required of Israel.

Thirdly, it is possible to use the term covenant to capture a sense of mutual obligation or contract between the two (respectively human and divine) partners, both of whom owe debts to each other. Here what is stressed is that God's relationship with Israel takes the form of a contract. God chose Israel and promises to be their God: Israel in turn must remain loyal to God and do as he tells it. The model here is possibly a political treaty, in which the overlord promises to protect his vassal provided that the vassal remains loyal and does not try to pursue independent policies. In the twentieth-century discussion of the concept of covenant many scholars pointed to ancient vassal-treaties as the models that the religious teachers of Israel were imitating in describing Israel's relation to its God in covenantal terms. But we could broaden the discussion by saying that after all a treaty is only a subset of a contract, and all contracts work on the basis that both parties must serve each other's interests, and not infringe the terms of the agreement between them.

The question then arises of when this contractual idea of the relationship between God and Israel first appeared. The modern consensus has increasingly come to be that it is not, as the Hebrew Bible portrays it, something that goes back genuinely to either Abraham or Moses (even supposing we really knew anything about those shadowy figures), but that it probably originated in the teaching of the eighth- and seventh-century prophets: Amos, Hosea, Isaiah, Micah, and Jeremiah. The prophets speak as though most people in their day thought of Israel's relationship with its God as an automatic one: God was by nature Israel's God and could be expected to be on her side. On the contrary, said the great prophets, God is only with you while you are with him. If you break his laws, then you are breaking your side of a bargain with him, and you can expect to take the consequences. The idea that God's relationship with Israel was contractual in character was then *read back* into an earlier period. Abraham did not simply receive a promise from God: he was also placed under an obligation to 'walk with God and be perfect', and to be circumcised and to circumcise his descendants as a sign of their obedience to the covenant. The covenant with king David came to be seen as equally a contract: there are versions of the covenant between God and David, for example in Psalm 89, which stress that the covenant is not just a free gift but rather a set of obligations which David and his descendants must observe. And all the laws revealed to Moses on Sinai came to be interpreted as the terms of the covenant between God and Israel, where originally they had probably been more or less secular state laws.

That is the kind of process modern scholars think occurred to change the character of the covenant-concept in ancient Israel, and to establish it as contractual in nature. One consequence is that just as it was possible for Israelites to break the covenant and therefore to incur the penalties which always follow breach of contract, so it was possible on the other hand to envisage the covenant as something non-Israelites might sign up to. The prophet we call Trito-Isaiah, who produced much of Isaiah 56–66, and who worked in the late sixth or early fifth century, is able to say that foreigners who observe the Sabbath and 'hold fast to my covenant' will be accepted by God alongside Israelites (Isa. 56:6–8). The covenant, because it is a moral contract, can be observed by anyone, who will then become acceptable to God and be able to worship in the temple, because it is to be a house of prayer for all the nations. It was this universalistic potential in the covenant idea that the earliest Christians exploited, saying that Jesus had become a kind of gateway through which Gentiles too could enter into the heritage of Israel. But they did not, with the possible exception of the author to the Hebrews, argue that therefore the covenant had been taken away from the Jews, or that a new covenant was needed. It was not long, however, before such a supersessionist message began to be heard.

In the Hebrew Scriptures we may see a development of the covenant idea in various directions over time. Is there any kind of unified picture if we try to read the Hebrew Bible as a whole, ignoring questions of historical development? After all, this is how both Jews and Christians read it in the first century: they were not interested in the stages by which its ideas had come into being. I think that the picture that emerges from the finished Hebrew Bible is clearly that the covenant is primarily a matter of God's election of Israel, and that it does indeed have the nature of a contract between Israel and its God – a bargain which must be kept, or else dire consequences will

197

follow. How bad these can be is evident from the history of the Hebrew kingdoms in the books of Kings, which end with disobedient Israel exiled from its land because of its persistent apostasy from God (2 Kings 25.21).

But there is always the sense that visiting the consequences of breach of covenant on Israel cannot be God's final word. Beyond judgement, there is hope for renewal, because God is infinitely merciful, and his commitment to his people is never in doubt. The idea that God could actually abolish the covenant altogether and substitute some new arrangement with the human race is never envisaged in the Hebrew Bible. Jeremiah's 'new' covenant (Jer. 31.31) is not an exception to this, but is indeed the proof of it. For Jeremiah, the covenant is so important that when Israel has broken it God restores it in a new form, in which, by writing the law on the people's hearts rather than simply on tablets of stone, he ensures that they will be permanently enabled to keep it. The new covenant is not in Jeremiah the replacement of Israel's covenant with God through Abraham or Moses, but a solemn renewal of it on a better basis. It is not surprising, however, that early Christians latched on to the passage from Jeremiah as one way of describing their sense that in Jesus God had done something genuinely new. The idea that this new thing meant that he had abandoned his original relationship with the Jews was not at all necessitated by adopting this prophecy as a description of the new experience in Christ. But unfortunately it was all too conveniently easy to think this, once relations with the parent religion had soured and Christians came to want to assert their own independence from contemporary Judaism.

The main use of covenant language in modern theology has been, indeed, in the dialogue with Judaism. In recent years it has become one of the ways in which Christians try to *avoid* supersessionism in thinking about Judaism. One way is to argue that there is a single covenant, which God made with his people, the Jews, and that Christians are now through Jesus Christ incorporated into that covenant. In one of the recent new prayers in the Church of England's service books Anglicans seem to be going down that road when, in the prayer on Good Friday that used (in its *Book of Common Prayer* version) to pray for the conversion of the Jews, they now (in *Common Worship*) pray that Jews and Christians alike may be faithful to the covenant that both share:

> Let us pray for God's ancient people, the Jews, the first to hear his word – for greater understanding between Christian and Jew, for the removal of our blindness and bitterness of heart, *that God will grant us grace to be faithful to his covenant* and to grow in the love of his name.

The corresponding prayer in the modern Roman Catholic liturgy, on the other hand, prays equally for mutual understanding but asks simply that the Jews may be faithful to God's covenant, rather than associating Jews and Christians together under one covenant – possibly implying that there is *another* covenant which God has made with Christians.

The first, Anglican, approach might be felt to have its good side, from a Jewish perspective, in not suggesting that God has more than one covenant, and in maintaining simply that Christians have been admitted to it, too. This avoids any sense that the ancient covenant with the Jews has been replaced. Its downside, of course, is that it may seem rather presumptuous in implying that the original covenant is open to Christians to join in, rather than being the unique possession of Jews. The prayer slides into a 'we' that seems intended to include both Jews and Christians, and this may be felt to claim too much. The Catholic approach may seem better in that it treats Christians' relationship with God as essentially a separate issue from that of the Jews, as a kind of second or additional covenant. But the downside of that is that it can easily be understood as supersessionist, by presenting this new covenant as superior to or as replacing the old one. There thus are traps and pitfalls for the unwary in both ways of talking about covenant in the context of Jewish-Christian relations.

In all this, the idea of covenant itself tends to go unanalysed. It seems to me that the use of covenant language as a way of speaking about Christian relations with Judaism may suffer from the unrecognized possibility that Christians do not naturally use the language of covenant at all in thinking about their own relationship with God – and I want to suggest that this is also a considerable drawback in using it in the inner-Anglican context. It is true that the Christian Scriptures are called the New Testament, and that this implies a contrast with the Old Testament, such that some think this language supersessionist in itself. It is also true that in this way of speaking 'Testament' originally meant covenant, since *testamentum* is the word used to translate the Hebrew *berith* and Greek *diatheke* in Latin translations of the Hebrew Scriptures and of the New Testament. But very few Christians actually realize this. For the average Christian the word Testament is opaque, and means in practice a section of the Bible. Christians who talk of the Old or New Testament are not usually consciously thinking of the idea of a covenant at all. So even granted that it is from covenant language that the terms derive, that meaning is not apparent to the average Christian reader, who in hearing about Jewish-Christian relations does not understand why the language of covenant should be used at all, or what it has to do with the matter in hand.

When Christians are aware of the language of covenant, it is probably mainly from the Epistle to the Hebrews, which is perhaps the nearest to supersessionism of any book in the New Testament. It arises because Hebrews, in a passage traditionally read on Good Friday (10:1–18), speaks of the new covenant promised by Jeremiah in Jer. 31:31, and sees this prophecy as fulfilled through Christ. It contrasts this new covenant with the old covenant with Israel, which is now replaced by it. It is pretty clear that at least a surface reading of this text encourages supersesssionism, and Christians who know their New Testament (or at least this passage) will often talk freely of the way Christianity has replaced Judaism in the providence of God. But it is important to notice that the 'old' covenant of which Jeremiah speaks in this passage is the covenant made through Moses (cf. the quotation in Heb. 8:9 of Jer. 31:32: 'the covenant that I made with their ancestors on the day when I took them by the hand to lead them out of the land of Egypt'). When they think of the covenant between God and the Jews, therefore, Christians tend to think of Moses, and to have in mind that Jesus replaces Moses as the leader of a new religion.

But Jews do not at all think first of Moses when they hear the term covenant, but of Abraham: after all, the ancient Hebrew term *berith*, pronounced 'brit', serves in modern Judaism as a shorthand term for circumcision – the sign not of any covenant made through Moses, but of the relationship inaugurated with Abraham. It is the Abrahamic covenant that is in question in Judaism, but the supposed Mosaic one that Christians are often thinking of. This is bound to lead to a measure of mutual misunderstanding. When they speak of themselves as the beneficiaries of a new covenant, therefore – though such language, as we have seen, is not all that common anyway in inner-Christian discourse – Christians have in mind the Pauline idea of Christ as replacing the Torah, the law given through Moses, as the way of life which God's people should follow. They generally are not thinking of a replacement for the choice of Abraham by God. Thus what seems like a shared term, and therefore a good basis for dialogue between the two faiths, turns out to obscure more than it clarifies. It is only those Jews and Christians who engage in interfaith dialogue who tend to use the word 'covenant' to describe the relationship of their community to God at all. Thus it becomes part of a kind of private language of Jewish-Christian ecumenism, not really in touch with the way either of the two communities naturally thinks about itself. Any Christian who has been in dialogue with members of other churches will be aware of how easily such private languages can develop, and can lead to the use of special terms not much known to ordinary members of the churches in question. I would hazard a guess that 'primacy' and *episkope* are examples of this in inter-Christian discourse, and 'covenant' is certainly an example in Jewish-Christian relations.

None of this suggests that the language of covenant is likely to be all that useful in the present inner-Anglican crisis. As we have seen, it is used in the Old Testament to speak of the relationship between Israel and God, but this usage does not affect its occasional use for inner-human agreements, as in the covenant between David and Jonathan. There is nowhere in the Bible where the two usages are combined, so that the covenant between God and Israel means that Israelites are bound 'covenantally' to each other. To spell it out explicitly: the idea that 'the covenant relationship with God generates a covenantal relationship between his people' does not correspond to anything in the Bible. This is simply an attempt by those who want us to instigate an Anglican Covenant to add a patina of solemnity and holiness to a proposed agreement between human beings.

The background of the proposed inner-Anglican Covenant is not in fact biblical. It derives from the use of covenant language in the secular sphere, and in a number of modern inter-church agreements, for example, in current dialogue between the Church of England and the Methodist Church.

There is of course no reason why the term should not be used to signal that the intended relationship is a solemn matter, but it should not be supposed that it is somehow more 'biblical' to use this word than to speak of a binding agreement, a concordat, or a promise. My own fear is that employing the language of covenant is largely just a way of trying to raise the stakes. After all, if the term is biblical, and if the proposed agreement is called by a term hallowed by biblical usage, who can oppose it without opposing the Bible itself? But this risks being cant. The term is not being used in any recognizably biblical sense, and it is no more helpful in inner-Anglican than it is in Jewish-Christian discussion. Anglicans need to agree to go on talking to each other about the matters that divide them, and to do so honourably and straightforwardly. I doubt whether it helps this process to ask them to sign a 'covenant' to do so.

Index

Biblical References

Genesis
9.1–17	146
15.18	146
17	146
21	72
31	72

Exodus
6.7	64
20.1–17	147

Leviticus
26.12	64

Deuteronomy
26.17–19	64
29.12–13	64

2 Samuel
7	194
7.24	64

2 Kings
25.21	198

Psalms
25	194
89	196

Isaiah
56.6–8	197

Jeremiah
31.31	146, 198

Matthew
13.44	138

Mark
12.28–31	147

John
17.16	134

Acts
2.8	123

Romans
2	67
4.12	179
8.28	157
11.22–3	66
13.8–10	147

1 Corinthians
5	69
10.1–5	65
10.12	66
11.33	69
12.21	69
14	69

Ephesians
4.1–6	182

1 Thessalonians
5.13–24	61

Hebrews
8.9	201
10.1–18	201

Revelation
7.9	123